my first NEEDLE-FELTING BOOK

my first NEEDLE-FELTING BOOK

30 adorable animal projects
for children aged 7+

MIA UNDERWOOD

CICO Kidz

Published in 2019 by CICO Books
An imprint of Ryland Peters & Small Ltd
20–21 Jockey's Fields, London WC1R 4BW
341 E 116th St, New York, NY 10029

www.rylandpeters.com

10 9 8 7 6 5 4 3 2 1

Some material in this book was previously published in *My Felted Friends*, In 2012.

A CIP catalog record for this book is available from the Library of Congress and the British Library.

ISBN: 978 1 78249 708 0

Printed in China

Editor: Katie Hardwicke
Designer: Alison Fenton
Illustrator: Harriet de Winton, with additional illustrations by Cathy Brear
Photographer: Geoff Dann
Prop maker and stylist: Trina Dalziel

In-house editor: Dawn Bates
In-house designer: Eliana Holder
Art director: Sally Powell
Head of production: Patricia Harrington
Publishing manager: Penny Craig
Publisher: Cindy Richards

To see more of Mia Underwood's work, visit her website: www.miaunderwood.co.uk

Contents

Introduction

Needle felting is a great craft to learn—you don't need lots of equipment and it's easy to pick up and take with you if you're on vacation, on a car journey, or waiting at soccer practice! There are lots of ways to shape the wool fibers to create different animals, adding color and detail as your experience grows.

The animal kingdom is a fantastic place to find inspiration for felted animals. From wild animals and birds from every continent to pampered pets and farm animals from closer to home, we have chosen a whole menagerie of delightful characters. In Chapter 1, Wild and Wonderful, you can choose from monochromatic pandas and zebras, a cute polar bear cub, or the king of the jungle himself, the lion. In the next chapter, Feathered Friends, you can practice covering a polystyrene ball in wool to make a friendly robin or Easter chicken, or try the cute penguin chick. The colorful parrot uses flat-felting to make a beautiful hanging, covered in beads if you like sewing.

Chapter 3 heads for the countryside where you can find all sorts of critters, from cheeky squirrels and shy deer, to fluffy lambs and sly foxes. In the last chapter, Playful Pets, you can choose between dogs and cats, cute hamsters and bunnies, and even a sweet pony. It's easy to change the colors and markings to create a felted pet that resembles your family favorite, or just make one to keep you company or give as a gift.

Crafting with a needle may seem a little daunting at first, but follow the instructions in the Techniques section on pages 8–21, and build up your skills gradually. There are different project levels (see below), from easier and quicker level one projects to level three projects that use more complicated techniques.

The best place to begin is the Panda Patch (see page 24). This is a simple 2-D shape that uses flat felting to "color in" the panda's face, teaching you how to hold the needle and apply the wool. After this, you could go on to 3-D needle felting to make the lamb (see page 70) or the penguin (see page 50), then try a more colorful project. Soon you'll be creating any animal you like!

Project levels

Level 1
Simple projects that are relatively quick to make and use one or two colors with simple shaping

Level 2
Projects that use several colors and involve more detailed modeling and shapes

Level 3
Projects that take the most time to complete as they use several colors and detailed patterns, and some include limbs

Materials

You only need four things to get you started: a felting needle, foam block, wool fibers, and embroidery scissors.

Felting needle and handle

Use 36- and 38-gauge triangular needles for the projects.

Wool fibers

Made from wool in a range of textures. Don't cut the fibers—pull them off (see below).

Wefts and wisps

You will use wefts and wisps of wool to make your animals. Simply pull different amounts of wool off the coil with your fingers:

A generous weft Hold the bulk of the coil of wool fiber with one hand and wrap your other hand in a fist firmly around the end. Pull hard on the end and the fistful of wool that comes away is a generous weft.

A weft Hold the end of the wool in your palm, gripping it between your fingers and your palm. Pull on the end to pull off a weft of wool.

A wisp Grip part of the end of the wool between your forefinger and thumb, and pull off a wisp of wool.

Foam block, pad, or mat

Use a dense foam block about 1½in (4cm) deep as a base to needle on to.

Embroidery scissors

Use small, sharp scissors to trim shapes, snip off unwanted fuzz, or to style hair tufts and whiskers.

Other items

Measuring tape or **ruler** Use to check the sizes of the needle-felted shapes used to build your animal.

Beads, beading needle, sewing needle, and black sewing thread If you are adding beads or want to sew on a brooch finding.

Paper for templates, **scissors, ready-made felt,** and a **fabric pencil or chalk** for marking shapes onto felt.

Chenille stems (pipe cleaners) and **metal skewers** to make posable limbs.

Carding combs or **dog brushes** to comb and prepare natural fleece.

OUCH! NEEDLE SAFETY

Felting needles are very sharp and you may accidentally stab yourself when using the needle for the first few times. Remember to take your time, keep calm, and work at a steady, relaxed pace, keeping your eye on the needle at all times. Keep your needles in a safe storage box to prevent accidentally hurting yourself or others.

Techniques

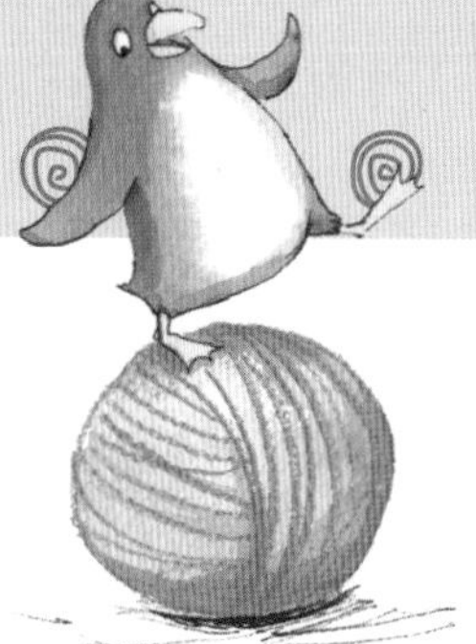

Needle felting works by turning soft, fluffy wool into a firm shape. When you stab the wool with the needle, the barbs on the needle move the wool fibers so that they tangle and bind together.

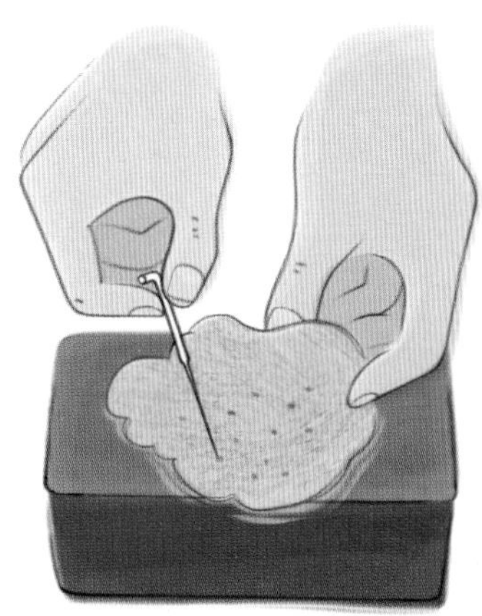

With just one felting needle you can create all the animals in this book! Practice the basic technique of stabbing the wool fibers on a foam block before you start the projects. Stab the fibers in the same way that a sewing machine needle works, up and down, turning the mass of fibers as you needle to create a 3-D shape. The needles are quite fragile; you can insert a needle at any angle into the fibers, but you must bring it up at the same angle or you might snap the needle.

Making basic shapes

The bodies and heads of all the animals are made from balls or egg shapes of wool fiber, and other simple shapes make tails, legs, necks, wings, and beaks. The bodies and heads do not need to be completely solid, just firm. Look closely at animals and try to recreate their shapes by squeezing in or padding out the felt (see page 13).

Bodies and heads

A large egg shape is the basis of all the animals' bodies, while a small egg makes most of the heads.

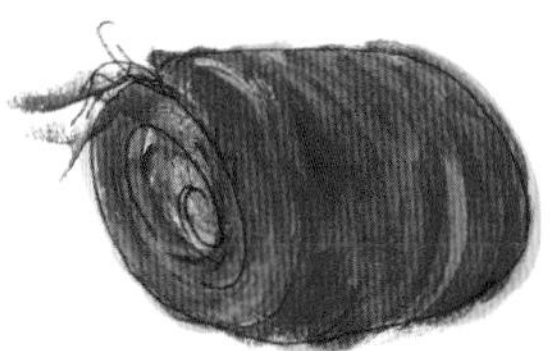

1 Pull off a generous weft for a body or a weft for a head (see page 7) and curl it into a roll. Place the roll on the foam block and needle the loose end to stop the roll uncurling.

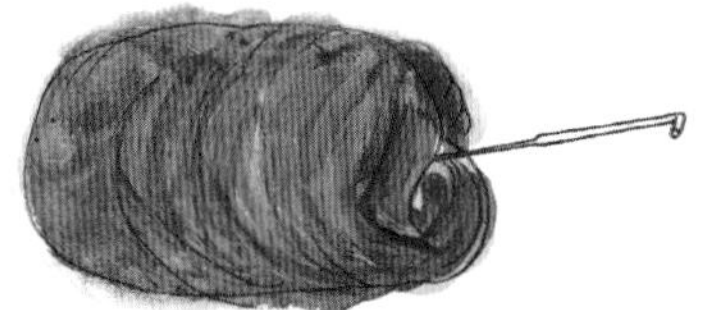

2 At one end, use the needle to push the curled ends in toward the middle to start forming the egg shape. Turn the roll in your hand as you work to make an even shape. Turn the roll around and repeat at the other end.

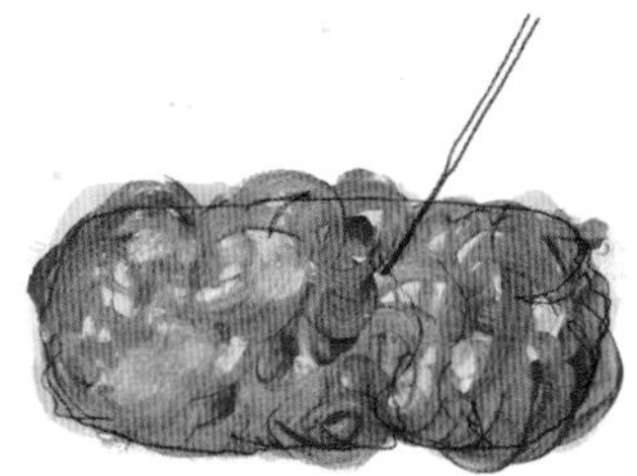

3 Lay the egg on the foam block. Needle it all over to bring in the loose fibers and firm up the egg shape, turning it as you work. Squeeze it into the shape you need with one hand while needling it with the other hand. To make a round ball, needle the ends in more firmly and roll it between your palms.

4 Check the size of the egg given in the project. If the egg needs to be smaller, keep needling it to shrink it. If it needs to be larger, pull off a weft or a wisp (see page 7) and wrap it around the egg. Hold the wool in place with one hand and lightly needle the wrapped ends to the egg to attach them. Needle it all over until the wool is smoothly blended in. Repeat until the egg is the required size.

Legs and tails—sausage shape

Part of the sausage will be felted and part will be left as loose fibers so that it can be attached to another piece.

1 Fold a weft or wisp of wool in half, lay it on the foam block, and needle the fold to stop the weft unfolding.

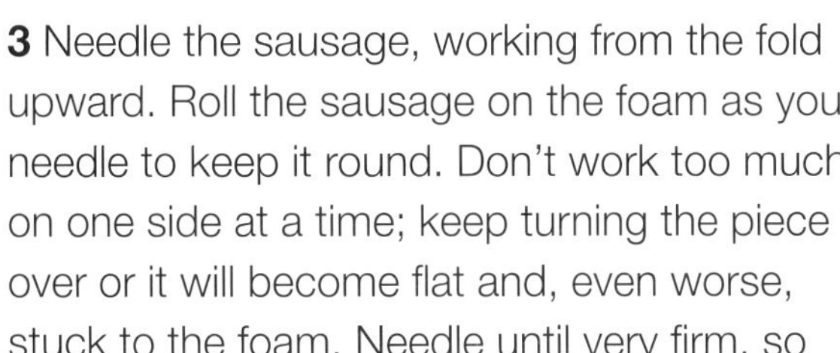

2 Curl in both of the sides of the folded weft to create a sausage shape.

3 Needle the sausage, working from the fold upward. Roll the sausage on the foam as you needle to keep it round. Don't work too much on one side at a time; keep turning the piece over or it will become flat and, even worse, stuck to the foam. Needle until very firm, so that the animal can stand up. For legs and arms, check the project for how long the felted section should be, and leave about half that length again as loose fibers at the top to attach it with. Tails need about one-third of the felted length to attach them.

4 Take the sausage off the foam block and roll it between your palms to bring in any loose fibers and keep the shape rounded. Check the measurements; if it needs to be fatter, then wrap a wisp around it and felt it on as for a body. If the sausage needs to be longer, then add a folded wisp to the folded end.

Ears, tails, and wings

Flat pieces of various shapes and sizes are what make ears, some tails, and wings. Sometimes these shapes will need to have loose fibers at one end for attaching them; at other times, they are finished off and attached in another way.

1 Fold or curl a weft or wisp of wool into roughly the shape you need. Place it on the foam block and needle it lightly to make the rough shape.

2 Roll in the edges and any loose fibers at the folded end and needle them down. Then needle all over to shape it, leaving the fibers at the open end loose. Turn it over to needle the other side.

3 If loose fibers are not needed to attach the piece, then fold them over and needle them into the shape.

4 Check the measurements in the project, then take the piece off the foam and needle around the outside to make a more defined edge.

Necks and beaks

The animals based on Basic Body 1 (see page 14) need a neck formed from a cone. Much smaller cones are used to make bird's beaks.

1 Curl a weft or wisp into a cone shape and lightly needle the loose ends to stop it uncurling. Then lightly needle the whole cone to form the shape.

2 For a long neck, wrap another weft around the bottom end to extend the cone. Needle into place.

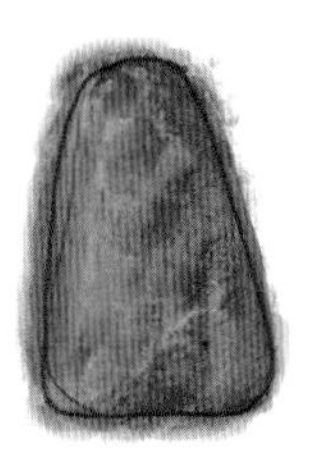

3 Needle in the base, pushing in all the loose fibers until it is flat. Needle the surface until the cone is firm, then check the measurements. Add more wefts or wisps if the cone needs to be larger, or needle it more to shrink it. If the piece is a beak, pinch and needle the point.

Joining basic shapes

Once you have made the separate parts of an animal's body, you need to join them together.

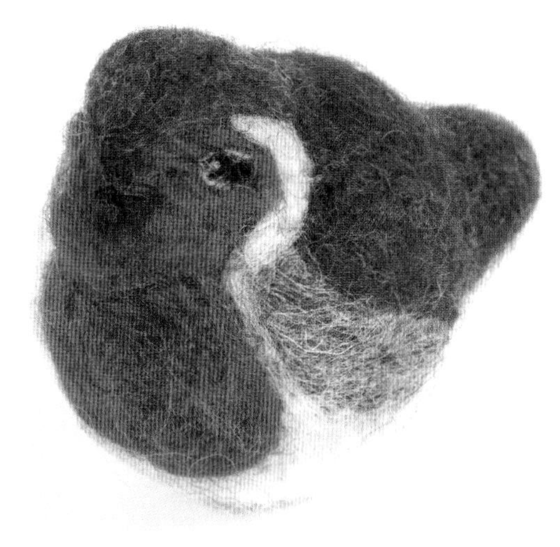

Head to body

This usually means joining one egg shape to another egg shape.

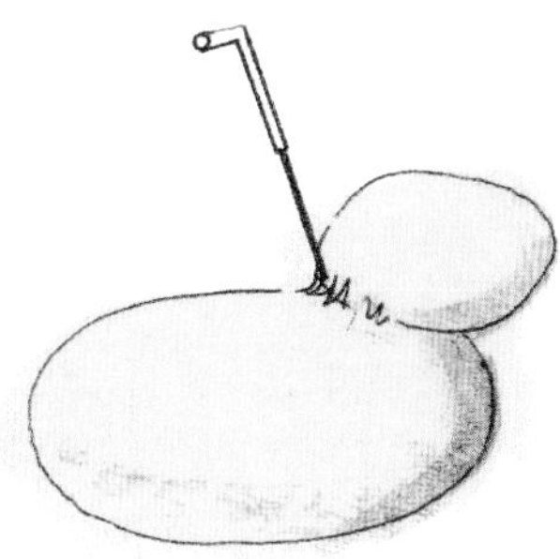

Hold the pieces in position with one hand. Push the needle through one edge of the smaller egg into the other egg, then take it out to fuse the two pieces. Work all around the edge of the smaller egg where the two pieces meet, until they are joined together. See page 12 to blend the join.

Leg or tail to body

Here, you are joining a sausage piece to an egg shape, using the loose fibers left at one end of the sausage.

1 Position the sausage on the egg shape and wrap the loose ends over the egg. Hold the pieces together with one hand and needle the loose fibers lightly to baste them to the egg.

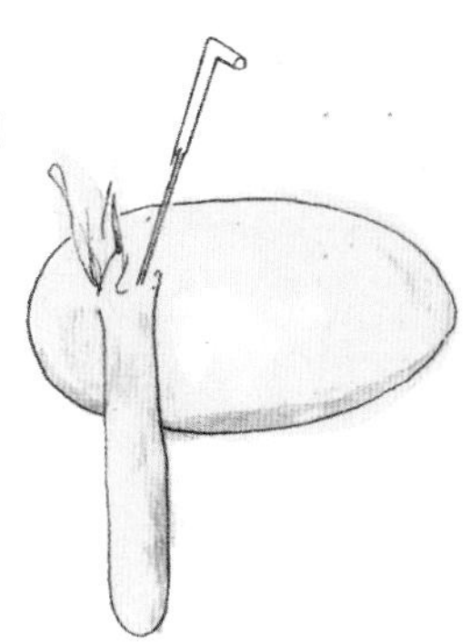

2 Needle all the loose fibers until the sausage is firmly joined on.

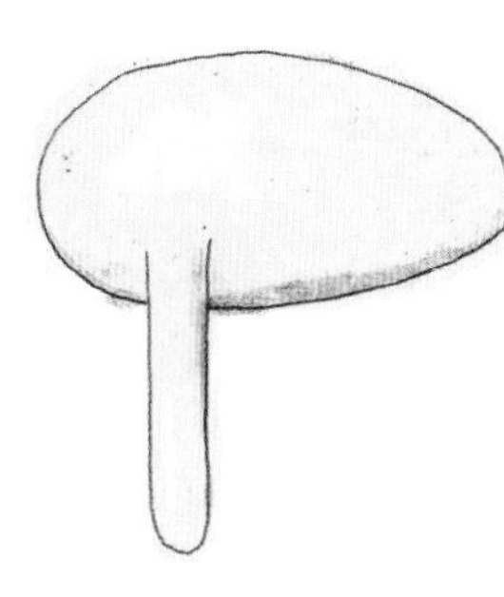

Wing or ear to body

These pieces do not have loose fibers to join them on with.

1 Position the flat piece on the egg shape and hold them together with one hand. With your other hand, push the needle through one edge of the flat shape into the egg, then take it out to fuse the pieces. Work around the edge of the flat shape until it is joined on.

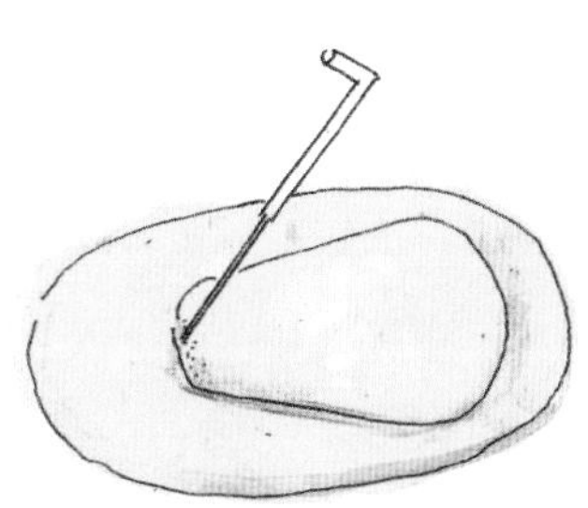

Neck or beak to body or head

A large cone (for a neck) or a small one (for a beak) are attached to a body or head in the same way as other solid shapes are joined.

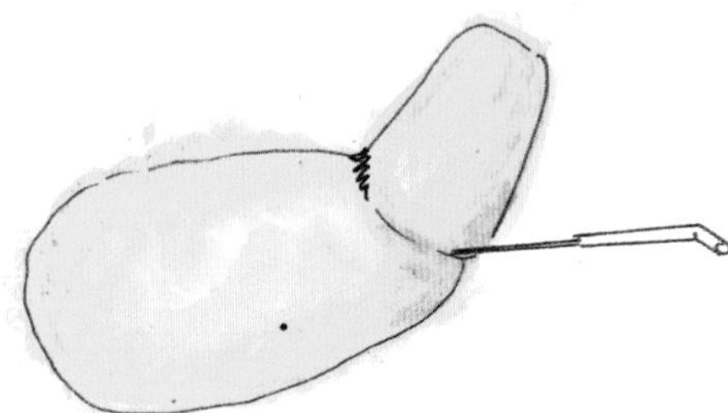

1 For a neck, position the cone on top of the narrow end of the egg, holding it in place with one hand. With your other hand, push the needle through the edge of the cone into the egg, then take it out to fuse the two pieces. Work all around the edge of the cone until it is joined on, turning the piece all the time to check that the neck is at the correct angle. Do the same to attach a beak.

SMOOTHING THE SURFACE

After joining and blending pieces you may be left with wisps of wool lying in different directions, and sometimes with unwanted lumps and bumps. To smooth these out, lay a weft over the whole area, tucking it loosely around the shape. Hold the weft in place while needling evenly all over it until the surface is smooth. Needle in any contours (rounded shapes) you want to keep.

Blending joined shapes

Once two shapes have been joined together, the join needs to be blended and strengthened with more wefts of wool.

Leg or tail to body join

It is important that this join is strong, so that the animal can stand upright.

1 Wrap a weft or wisp of wool under and around the leg, crossing the ends over on the outside top of the leg, at either the front shoulder or rear haunch. To strengthen a join, pull off a long wisp and wrap it right around the top of the leg before crossing the ends. Needle the whole wisp until it is smooth. Repeat to build up the area.

2 A tail is blended in a similar way to a leg join. Wrap a weft or wisp of wool under and around the tail, crossing the ends over on the bottom of the animal's back. You can adjust the position of the wrapped weft to shape the body or add height to the back. Needle all around to blend the two shapes.

Padding shapes

Once a basic body is created, it will need to be padded and molded to create the right shape.

1 Curl a weft or wisp into roughly the shape required. Hold the curled wool in place on the area you want to pad out. Needle all around the edges first to make the shape, then needle over the whole area.

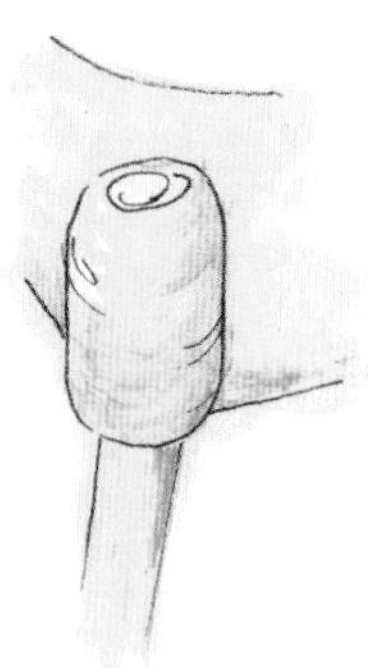

2 Work lightly to start, needling more to firm up the padding as the shape becomes clearer. Add another curled wisp or weft to pad out the area further if needed.

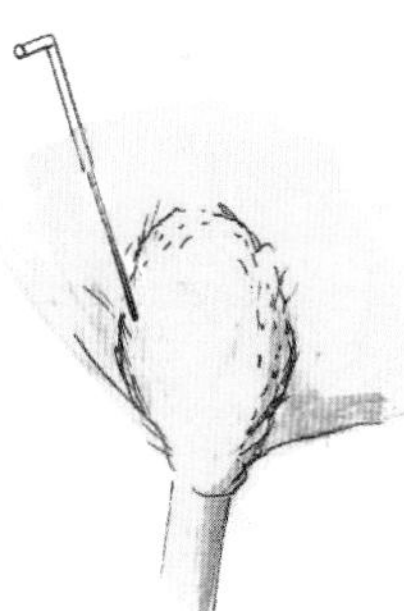

Extending shapes

It is better to build up a shape gradually, so add a few wisps at a time, rather than a single big weft, until the desired shape is achieved.

1 Wrap a wisp or weft around the end of the shape you want to make bigger. Hold the wrapped wisp in place with one hand.

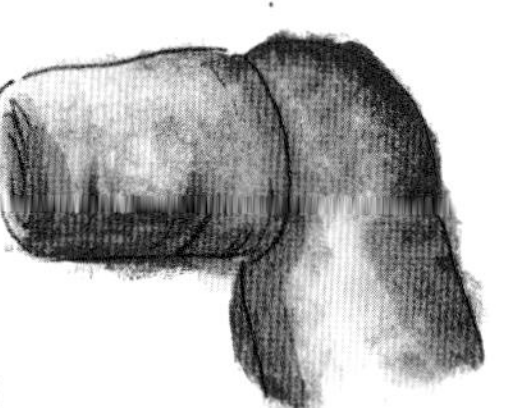

2 Needle the wisp around the base first—where it is wrapped around the existing shape—and work the needle outward. Pinch in the piece if you need to shape it. Needle all around until smooth. Add more wisps until the piece is the desired shape and proportion.

Shaping pieces

As well as adding wool to shape an animal, you can pinch and squeeze while needling to add contours (rounded shapes).

1 To shape a muzzle, pinch the tip of the head with one hand, and needle the muzzle where it is pinched to bring the shape in. To create the nose and mouth, pinch in both sides of the cheeks and the nose and mouth details.

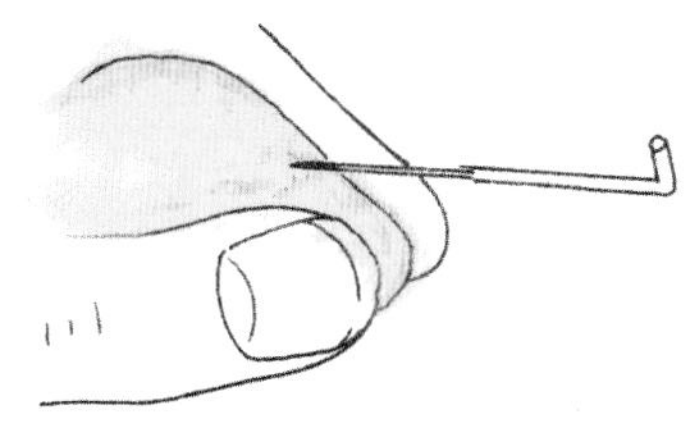

2 To shape larger areas, squeeze with all the fingers on one hand to bring the shape in where you'd like it to curve inward. With the other hand, needle into the entire area your fingers have squeezed, being careful not to prick yourself.

Basic body 1

Many of the animals share basic shapes and are put together in similar ways. Basic Body 1 is used for the dachshund, pony, deer, lion, and zebra.

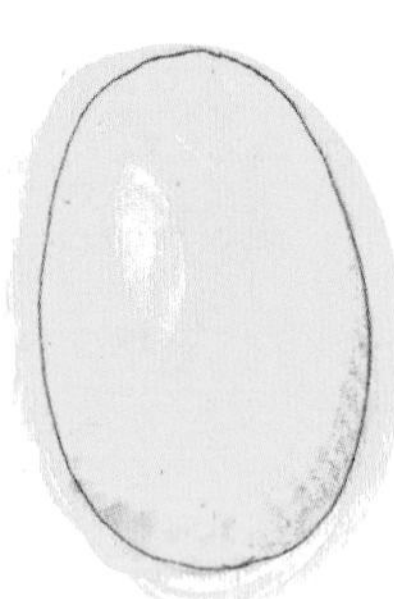

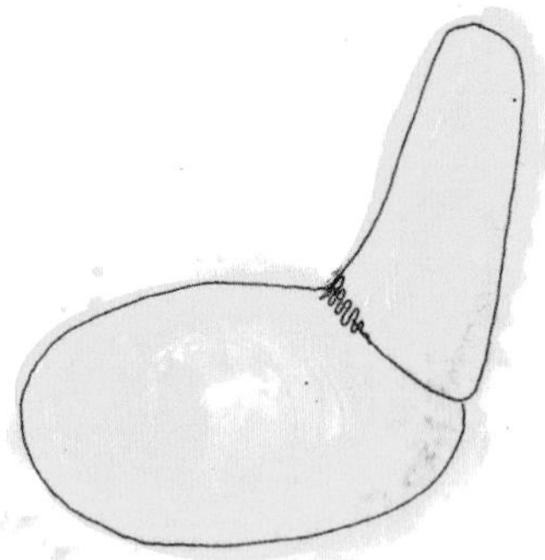

1 Start by making an egg shape for the body, making it the size and shape given in the project. The narrow end will be the beginning of the neck and the other end the animal's rear.

2 Wind a small weft of wool into a cone and needle it to make a neck. Add more wefts of wool to make the neck the required size, then join it to the body. Lay a weft of wool across the base of the neck, overlapping the top of the back, and needle it on to blend the neck into the back.

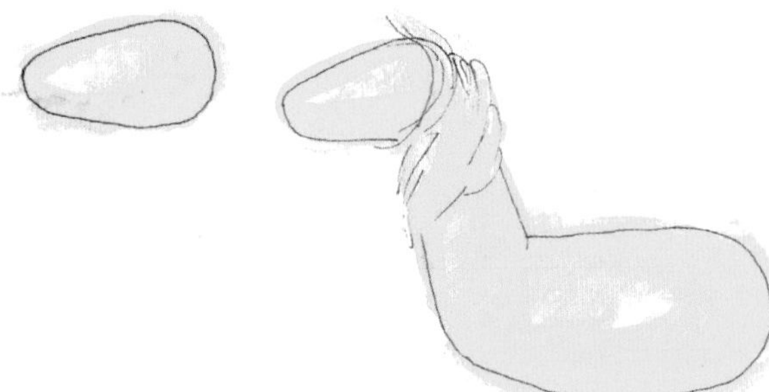

3 Make an egg for the head to the size and shape given in the project. Position the larger end of the head on top of the neck and join it on. Wrap a weft of wool over the top of the head and neck and around under the chin, and needle it in place to blend the head into the top of the neck.

4 Pull off four equal-sized wefts of wool and make four legs, making them the length given in the project and leaving loose fibers at the top. Put each leg on the foam block and work the needle all around the ankle, pinching it in while you needle until the lower leg is quite solid. Keep turning the leg so that you don't flatten it (or needle it to the pad). Shape the foot by needling and squeezing.

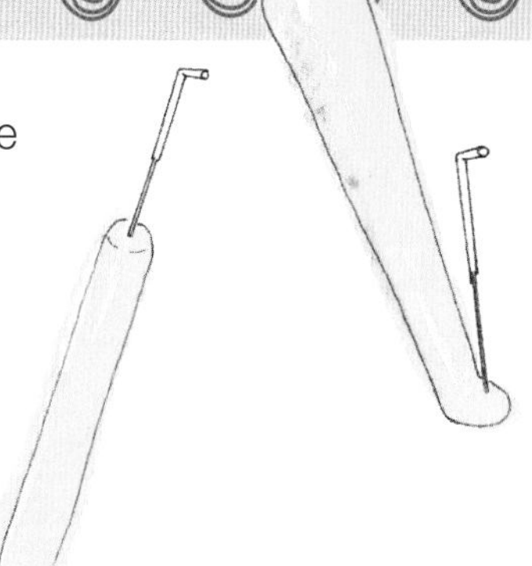

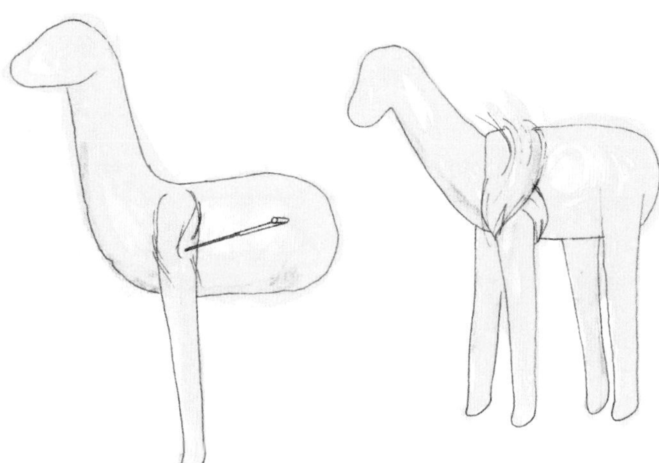

5 Attach the legs to the body, positioning them following the project instructions. Make sure all the legs are level so that the animal doesn't topple over. Wrap wisps of wool around the tops of the legs and needle them on to make the legs stronger and blend in the joins. Check that the animal stands level.

Basic body 2

This body shape is used for the badger, cheetah cub, panda, polar bear cub, Super-cute Yorkie, kitten, and bunny.

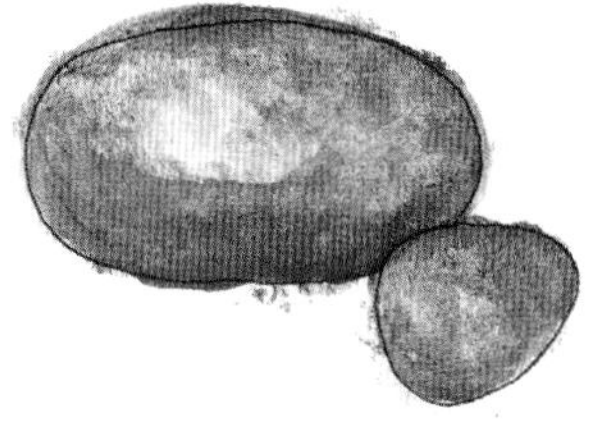

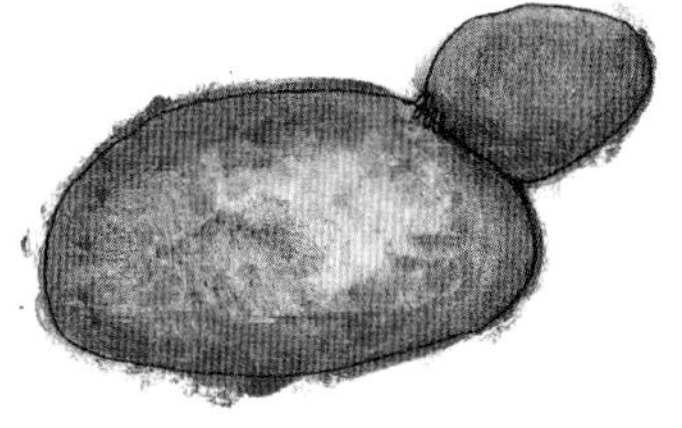

1 Start by making an egg shape for the body, making it the size and shape given in the project. The narrow end will be the beginning of the neck and the other end the animal's rear. Make a small egg shape for the head, as directed. This basic body does not have a neck step, so the head is added directly to the body. Attach the head just above the narrow end of the body.

2 Pull off a weft of wool and wrap it around the join like a scarf. Needle this in until it is smooth, then add another weft to the back, overlapping the neck area to blend the back of the head to the top of the body. Lay a wide weft over the neck, head, and back and wrap it around the chest. Needle this in to make the body's contours smooth and plump.

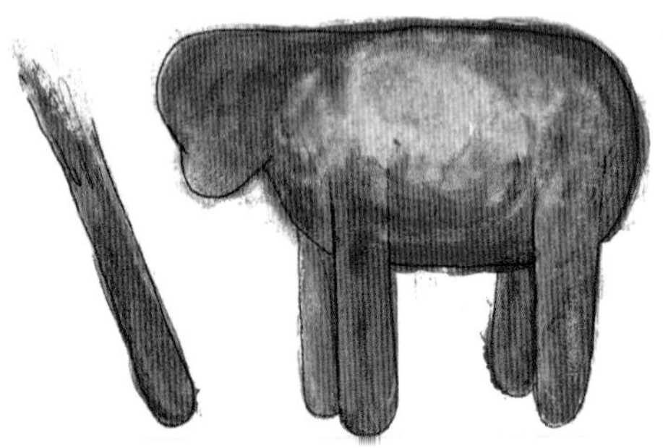

3 Pull off four equal-sized wefts of wool and make four legs, making them the length given in the project and remembering to leave loose fibers at the top to attach them with. Attach the legs to the body, positioning them following the instructions in the project. Strengthen and blend the leg joins as for Basic Body 1. Make sure that the legs are level and the animal stands on all fours without toppling.

Basic body 3

This is the body used for the duck, parrot, penguin, and owl.

1 Start by making an egg shape for the body, making it the size and shape given in the project. The narrow end will be the top and the fat end the base of the body. To add wings, pull off a piece of wool and lay it on the body where the wing is to be. With the felting needle, push in the loose fibers around the edges of the wing piece and guide them into the correct shape (see page 10). Repeat to place a wing on the other side of the body. (If you don't feel confident doing this, you can make flat wing shapes on the foam block and then attach them.) Turn the body to check that the wings are positioned correctly. Once you are happy with the position, lightly needle felt the whole wing to the body, keeping the profile rounded and adding more wool if it starts to look flat.

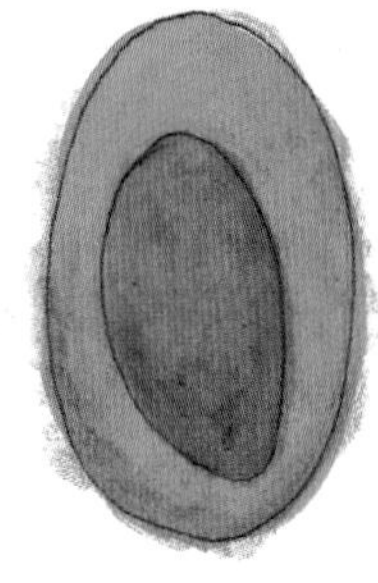

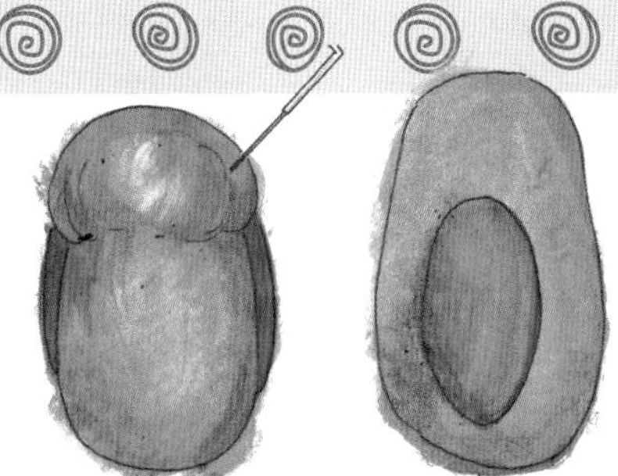

2 Fold a generous weft of wool in half and lay it on the top of the body, with the folded end at the front. Needle the fold to the body to outline the lower edge of the head. Turn the body around and needle in the loose fibers, so that the back of the head blends smoothly into the back of the body. Needle the whole head lightly into shape. Add more wefts of wool, keeping the head shape correct, until the head is the right size.

3 Fold a weft of wool in half and needle it into the size and shape given in the project for the tail. Needle on another layer of wool to stiffen the shape further. Hold the tail in position against the body, with the loose fibers running up the back. Needle the fibers onto the back. Needle around the base of the tail to attach it firmly to the body.

Flat felting

Flat felting means building up a shape on a flat piece of ready-made felt—like painting a picture rather than sculpting a 3-D shape.

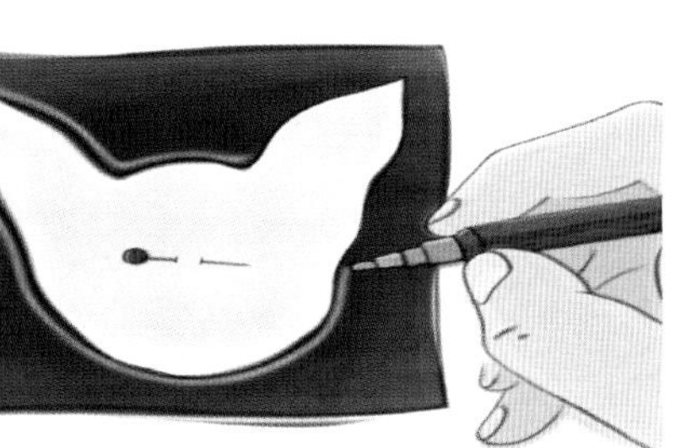

1 Copy the template onto paper and cut it out. Pin the template on the piece of felt, leaving a small margin around the edges. Using a pencil, marker, or a chalk pen, draw around the template, making sure that the pen marks are easy to see.

2 Put the felt piece on the foam block. Following the instructions in the project, take a weft or wisp of wool to fill in the shape and needle it in place, moving the needle up and down until the fibers have become attached to the felt.

Needling wool around a skewer

Long, slim, posable legs can be made by felting a tube, then poking a chenille stem (pipe cleaner) through it. The process first involves felting wool around a metal skewer to make the tube.

1 Pull off a long wisp of wool. Hold one end of the wisp in place at the top of the skewer and wrap the wool diagonally down it.

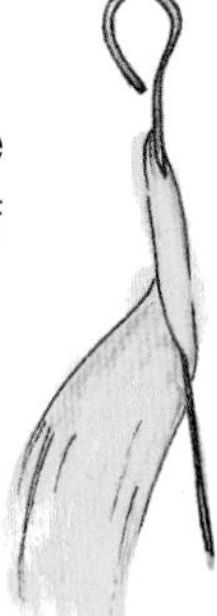

2 Lay the wrapped skewer on the foam block and needle it all over to felt the wool. Work lightly, pushing the needle in at an angle to avoid hitting the skewer too hard and damaging the needle. Roll the wrapped skewer between your palms to help felt any loose fibers. Keep needling and rolling until the wool is quite firmly felted.

3 Pull the skewer a short way out of the felted tube and push a chenille stem down the other end until it touches the skewer. Continue to pull out the skewer and push in the stem until the skewer is completely pulled out and the chenille stem runs right through the tube. If the stem gets stuck, pull it out and re-insert the skewer, then felt the wool tube a bit more. Bend the tip of the stem over by a small amount, pull the felt just over the folded tip, and needle it to hold it in place. If necessary, bend and cover the other end in the same way. Needle the whole piece lightly.

Applying color

There are various ways of adding color to your animals, either a solid background color or tones of a color, blending into one another.

Background color

Lay a weft or wisp of wool in position where you'd like to add the color and needle it lightly to roughly hold it on. Needle the loose fibers into the area you'd like to fill with the color, then needle the area until it is smooth.

Blended color

Pull off a wisp of wool of the color you would like to blend into the background color, and separate it into smaller pieces. Lay a small piece on the background and lightly needle it on, so that some of the background color shows through. You can soften the effect by adding a few strands of the background color on top of the blending color; this works well around the edges of colored patches. Add small amounts of different tones to create a mottled effect.

Precise color

To add stripes or spots requires a more precise technique. The amount of wool you use depends on the size of the spot, but it's easy to add more if necessary. You can use these techniques for larger areas of precise color, too, such as the pink inside ears.

Dots and spots

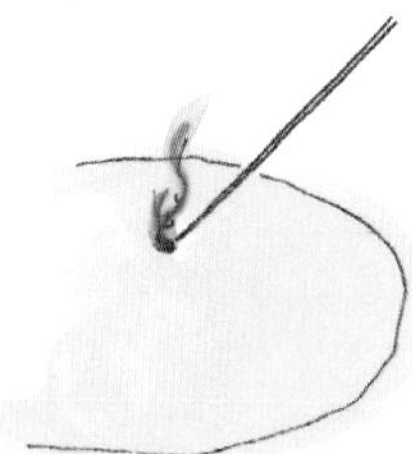

1 Hold a few strands of wool in place with your fingers and use the needle to poke the ends into the right place on the body.

2 Turn the needle clockwise to twist the loose ends of the fibers around the shaft, then poke the needle into the same place, taking the twisted fibers with it. Poke the needle in a few more times to anchor the spot, then twist to tuck in any loose strands.

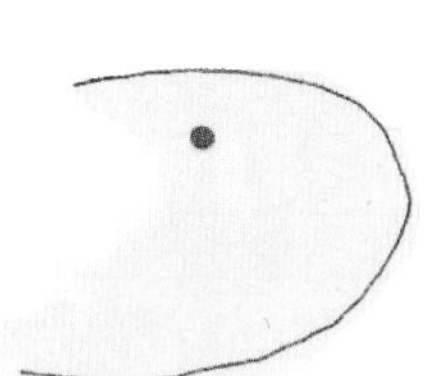

3 If you poke the needle in too hard, the spot can disappear. If this happens, just get a bit more wool and start again.

Stripes

You can use wisps of varying lengths and thicknesses to make your stripes more natural looking.

1 Pull off a wisp of wool of the stripe color. Hold each end between your thumb and forefinger and twist the wisp into a loose strip for a soft stripe. A tighter twist will make a very precise stripe or line. Hold the twisted wool strip in place where you would like the line to start.

2 Use the fingers of one hand to position and guide the strip, while using the needle in a sewing-machine motion to needle it into place. Poke loose fibers in with the tip of the needle, then rotate the needle above the end of the stripe to gather any last loose fibers and poke them down into place. Do not needle the strip too hard or it will make a dent in the animal. Lightly needle the whole surface to smooth it.

Adding fluffy texture

Some of the animals have just a little light fluff somewhere on their heads or bodies, while others have wonderfully luxuriant fur. The technique is the same, no matter how much fluff you need.

Pull off a wisp of wool and separate it into small pieces. Pull out the strands with your fingers to fluff them up, then lay them in position on the animal. Lightly needle in one end of the group of strands. Repeat the process to build up the fluff to the required amount. Use your fingers to rub and tease the fluff into the shape needed, then, if necessary, lightly needle the strands to sculpt the fluff into place. If it doesn't look right, you can just pull it off and start again.

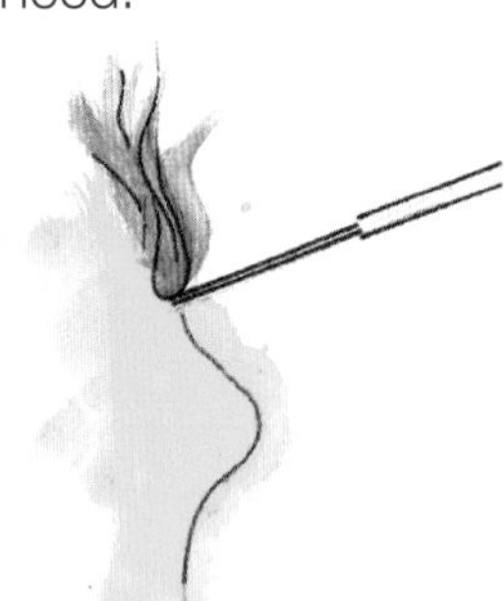

Making an eye

Many animals have an almond-shaped eye with a colored iris, black pupil, and a tiny white highlight but you can follow this method to make any style of eye. With every animal, it is the shape and angle of the white of the eye, the position and size of the iris and pupil, and the position of the highlight that give personality, so take a look at the photos before making the eyes. Try to make them identical or your animal may look oddly lopsided. If you make a mistake, just pull the wool off and start again.

1 First, make the white of the eye by very loosely rolling a small piece of white wool into a pea-sized ball. Hold it in place with a forefinger and thumb and poke the needle into it a few times to loosely attach it to the head. Then use the needle to guide the wool into an almond shape, needling it on around the edges as you go. Rotate the needle above the eye to gather in loose fibers as with a spot (see page 19), and needle them in to make the eye flat and solidly colored.

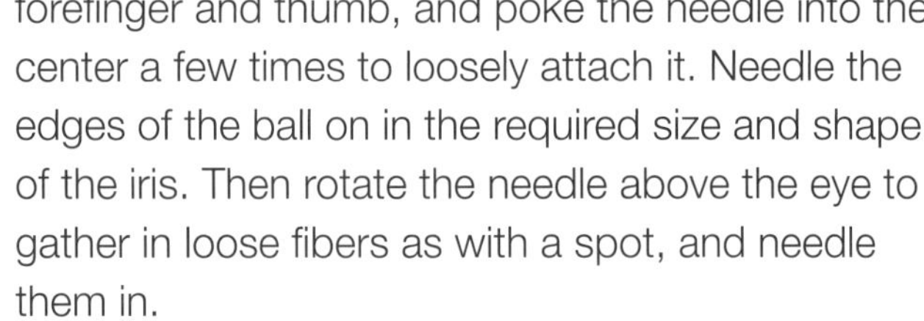

2 For the iris, roll a small piece of colored wool into a loose ball. Place it in position on top of the almond shape with your forefinger and thumb, and poke the needle into the center a few times to loosely attach it. Needle the edges of the ball on in the required size and shape of the iris. Then rotate the needle above the eye to gather in loose fibers as with a spot, and needle them in.

3 Use a little black wool to make a spot in the iris. Use just a few strands of white wool to make a dot for the highlight in the eye. Make sure that the highlight is in the same position in both eyes.

4 If the animal needs eyelids, needle on a short stripe above the eye.

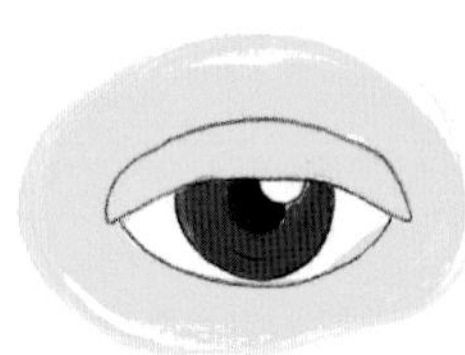

Adding ears

There are two kinds of basic ear—upright and flat. The projects will tell you what flat shape to make for an ear, and how to add the detail necessary for each animal. As with eyes, try to make the ears identical and symmetrically positioned or the animal can look lopsided.

Upright ears

These can be either pointed or rounded. If pointed, then the basic shape is usually a teardrop and the rounded end is attached to the head. Sharp points can also be trimmed into the final shape with scissors.

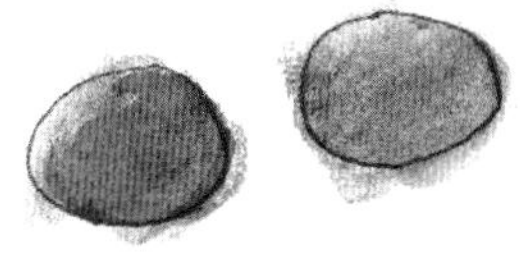

1 Create the two flat ear pieces as given for your animal. Do any shading on the ears as instructed.

2 Take one of the flat pieces and position it on the head with your forefinger and thumb. If the ear needs to be curved, then pinch the sides in as you hold it in place. Push the needle through the base of the ear where it meets the head, into the head itself, then take it out. Keep going to fuse the fibers around the back of the ear.

3 Needle in around the front of the ear in the same way to attach and shape it. If the ears are rounded, you can work the needle into the base of the back of the ear quite deeply to create the contour, then curl the top of the ear in by pinching it around the sides and needling in at the top.

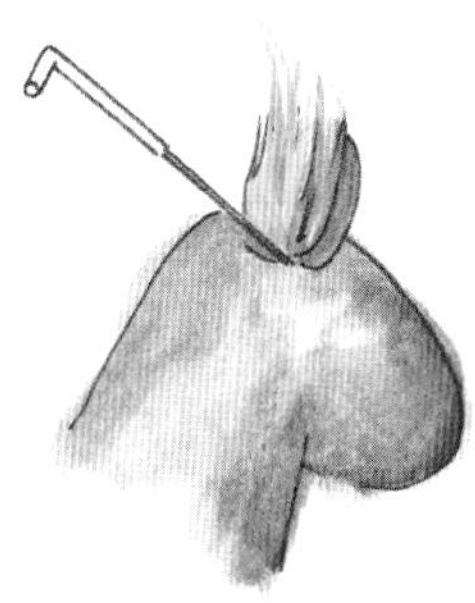

4 If required, add a folded wisp of wool to the back of the ear to blend it in, smooth over the join, and strengthen it. Now you can add any further coloring as instructed; pinch the ear while needling on the color to shape it if needed.

Flat ears

These ears are attached so that they hang down the sides of the animal's head.

Create the two flat ear pieces as given for your animal. Hold the ear against the head with your forefinger and thumb and needle through the top of the ear into the head: needle quite deeply, so that the ear is securely joined. Strengthen the join with a few strands of wool around the top and needle until smooth.

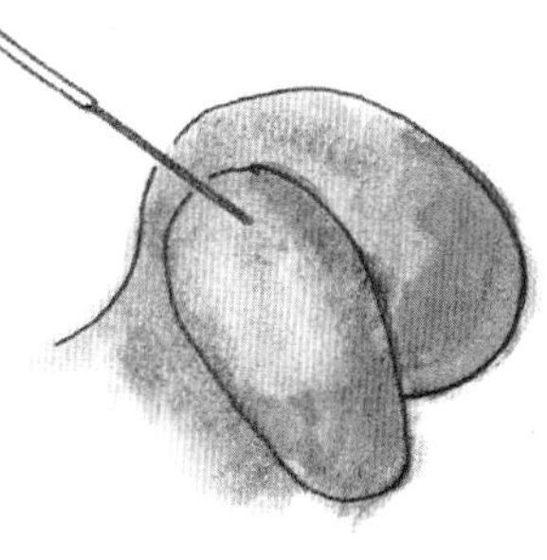

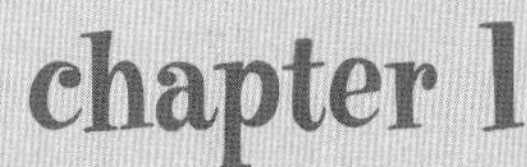

chapter 1

Wild and Wonderful

Panda Patch

Everybody loves a panda! This simple patch is quick to make and a great way of mastering your needling technique before moving on to the 3-D animals. It could be attached to a backpack or bag, either with fabric glue or hand stitching.

You will need

Template on page 126

3½ x 3½-in (9 x 9-cm) sheet of dark gray or black ready-made felt

Graphite pencil, marker pen, or fabric chalk

Merino wool in
black 0.07oz (2g)
white 0.18oz (5g)
pink 0.03oz (1g)

Felting needle with handle

Foam block or small felting mat

Sharp embroidery scissors

Techniques Checklist

Flat Felting page 17
Applying Color page 18
Making Basic Shapes: Ears, Tails, and Wings page 10
Making an Eye page 20

1 Copy the template on page 126 and cut it out around the outside of the shape. Place it on the gray or black felt and draw around the outside. Cut out the shape with sharp scissors. Put the felt shape in the center of the foam block or mat. To fill the face area with white, pull off a small wisp of white and place it roughly where you want it. Starting ⅛in (2mm) in from the outside edge, needle into the center until it is nice and even. Build up the color with wisps of white, filling in the whole area to create a solid-colored, smooth, flat surface (see page 17).

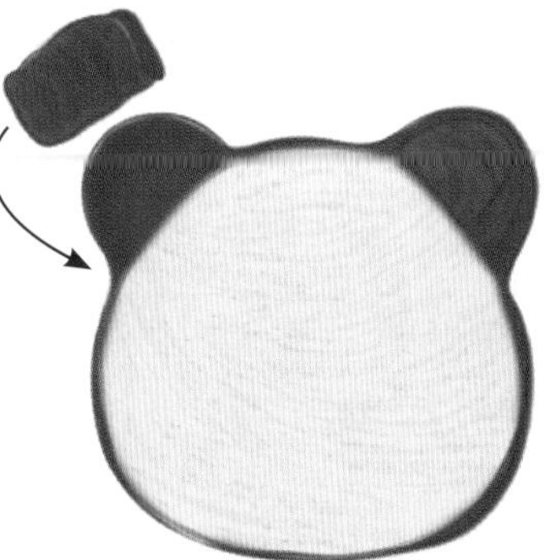

2 Take a wisp of black wool and fold it into a pillow shape (see page 10) and place it into position on the panda's ear. Needle the wool into place, making a definite shape and not going into the white area. Repeat for the other ear.

3 To help with the position of the face markings, use the template as a guide. Add a folded wisp of black for the patch around the panda's eye—build up the shape with small wisps so it doesn't get bulky. Repeat for the other eye. Add a rolled-up little ball of black for the nose and make a few stabs with the needle to hold it in place. Then work your way around the shape to create the outline of the nose before working the needle evenly over the shape. Try to keep the surface smooth and flat.

4 For the mouth shape, roll a small wisp of black wool between your fingers to create a very thin strip of wool. Start the strip from the middle bottom edge of the nose and work down carefully to make a short vertical line. Then get another little thin strip of black to create the small curved smile. Keep it even unless you want to change the expression of the face.

5 Using the template as a guide, roll a small wisp of white into a ball and place it on the black patch. Very carefully work your needle around the outer edge to create the oval shape for the whites of the panda's eyes. Repeat for the other eye. Then, with a very small pinch of black, roll it into a tiny ball and needle the black pupil into position (see page 20), using steady and slow strokes, being careful not to poke it too much or it might disappear. Take care to position the pupil in the center as this will give the panda its expression.

6 For the rosy cheeks, roll a small pinch of pink into a ball for each cheek and needle it evenly into place, trying to keep it flat.

7 Pull your panda patch off the felting block or mat and very carefully trim the furry wool off the reverse side and any long hairs on the face. You can also trim the narrow edge around the face to neaten it up or leave it as it is.

PRETTY as a picture!

Leopard Patch

Leopard print is always in fashion and this patch will add a touch of style to any bag or jacket. You can fix it on with fabric glue or sew it on by hand. It's another great 2-D project for developing needling skills and for practicing adding colored details to a project.

You will need

Template on page 126

4 x 4-in (10 x 10-cm) sheet of dark yellow felt

Graphite pencil, marker pen, or fabric chalk

Merino wool in
mustard yellow 0.18oz (5g)
white 0.07oz (2g)
black 0.07oz (2g)
orange 0.03oz (1g)

Felting needle with handle

Foam block or small felting mat

Sharp embroidery scissors

Techniques Checklist

Flat Felting page 17
Applying Color page 18
Making an Eye page 20

1 Copy the template on page 126 and cut it out around the outside of the shape. Place it on the yellow felt and draw around the outside. Cut out the shape with sharp scissors. Put the felt shape in the center of the foam block. To fill the whole area with mustard yellow wool, pull off a small wisp and place it on the felt. Starting ⅛in (2mm) in from the outside edge, needle in to the center until it is even. Build up the color with wisps of yellow, filling in the whole area to create a solid colored, smooth, flat surface (see page 17).

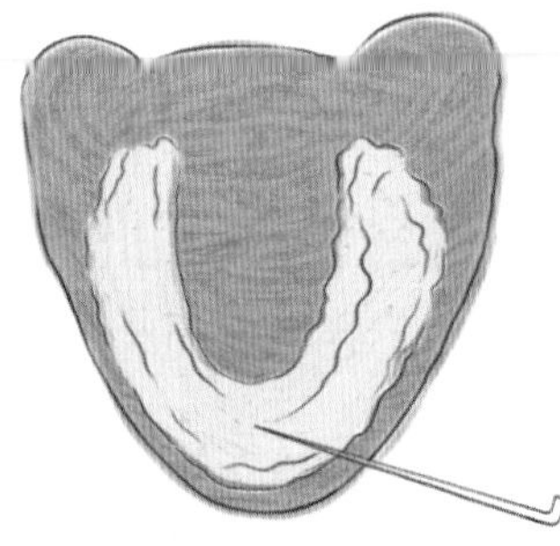

2 Pull off a generous wisp of white and fold it to create a "U" shape for the leopard's muzzle and eye area. Needle it in place, using the template as a guide for position.

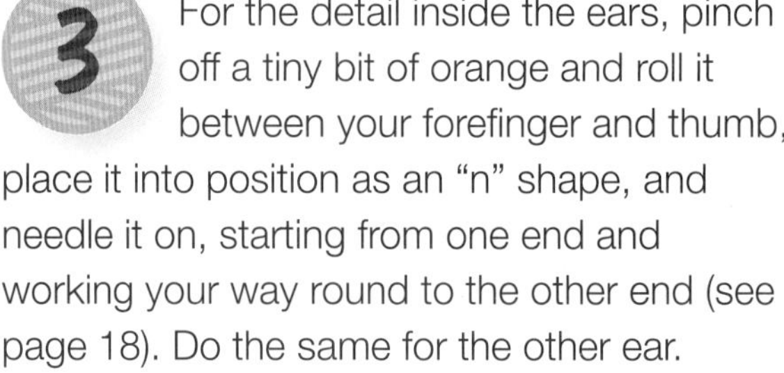

3 For the detail inside the ears, pinch off a tiny bit of orange and roll it between your forefinger and thumb, place it into position as an "n" shape, and needle it on, starting from one end and working your way round to the other end (see page 18). Do the same for the other ear.

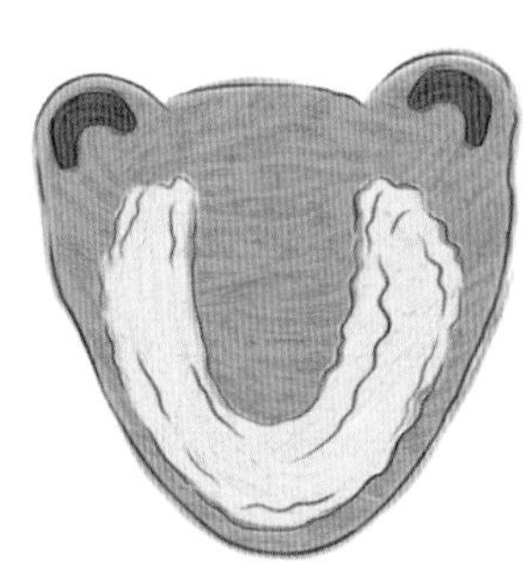

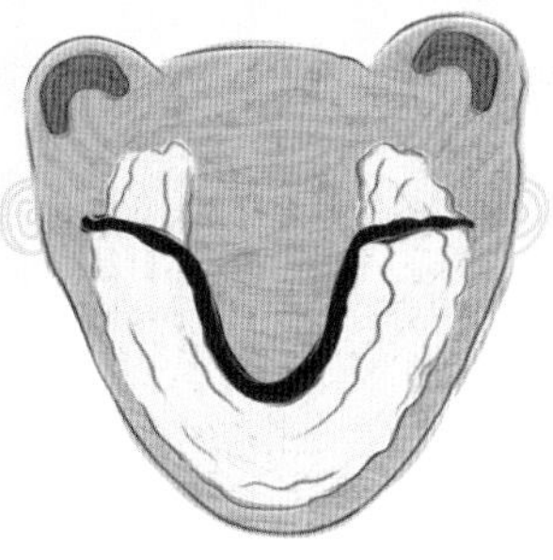

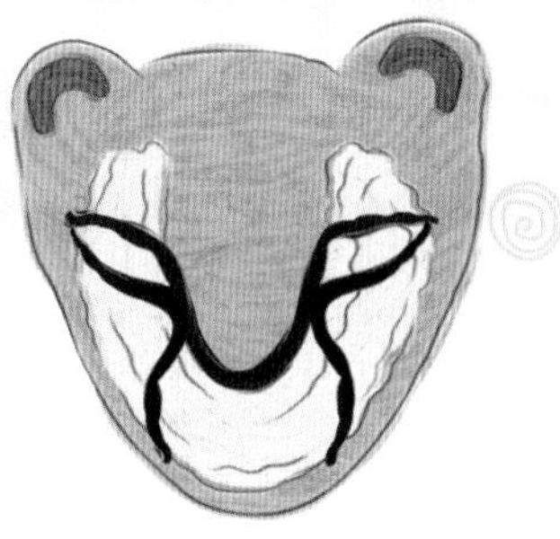

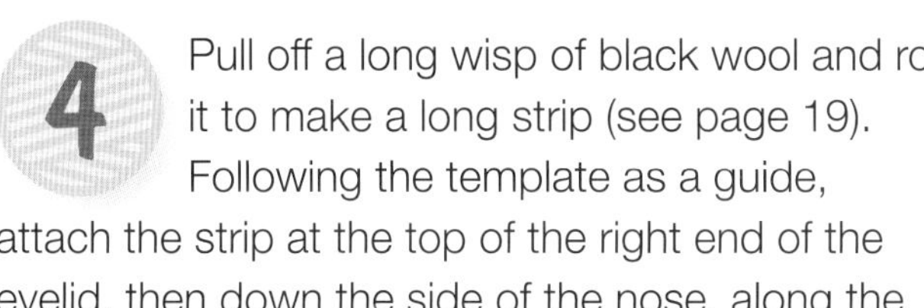

4 Pull off a long wisp of black wool and roll it to make a long strip (see page 19). Following the template as a guide, attach the strip at the top of the right end of the eyelid, then down the side of the nose, along the edge of the white "U" shape, needling it lightly to hold it in place, then back up the other side of the nose to the top of the left eyelid. Attach by needling steadily all along the strip. Now make another long strip of black wool and start from the tip of the right eye to create the bottom edge of the almond-shaped eye, continuing into the tear mark, and curving round to create the edge of the muzzle. Repeat for the other eye

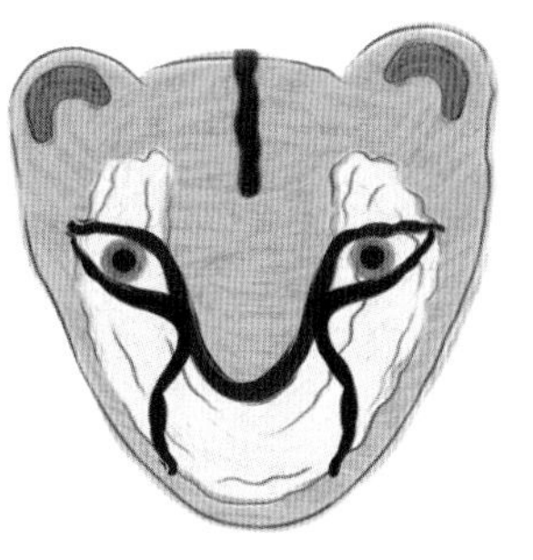

5 Pinch off a bit of orange, roll it into a small ball, and add it to the center of the white of the eyes (see page 20), to create the iris. Then add a pupil with a tiny pinch of black wool.

6 Add a little strip of black like a mustache, attaching it from the center of the strip to the tip of the nose, extending it to the sides for the mouth. Add a small ball of black for the nose, working the needle evenly until it is nice and smooth.

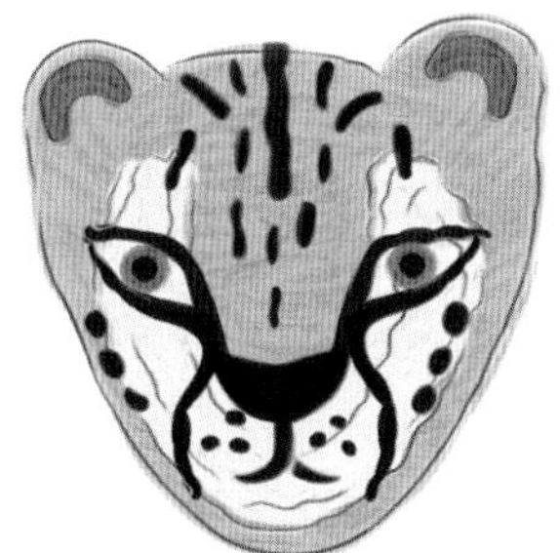

7 For the markings, pinch off tiny bits of the black wool and roll them to make short strips and dots (see page 19) and create a pattern. Follow the template or create your own unique pattern. Pull your leopard patch off the felting pad or mat and very carefully trim the furry wool off the reverse side and any long hairs on the face. You can also trim the narrow edge around the face to neaten it up or leave it as it is.

Catch me if you can!

Furry Bear Cub

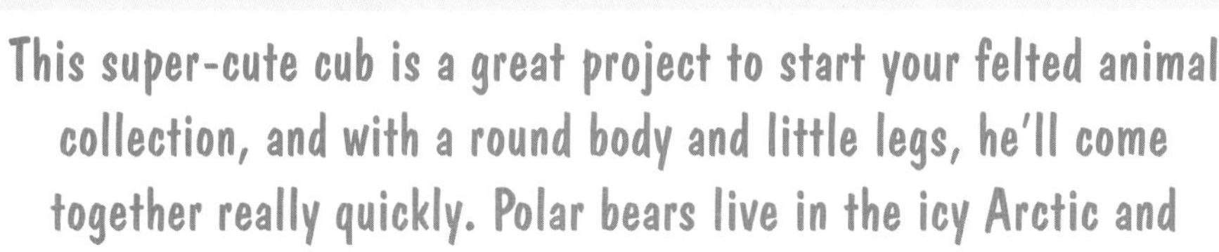

This super-cute cub is a great project to start your felted animal collection, and with a round body and little legs, he'll come together really quickly. Polar bears live in the icy Arctic and their fur isn't actually white, it's transparent!

You will need

Merino wool in
white 0.35oz (10g)
black 0.18oz (5g)

Carded sheep fleece in
white 0.70oz (20g)

Carded top wool in
dark gray 0.07oz (2g)

Felting needle with handle

Foam block

Sharp embroidery scissors

Techniques Checklist

Basic Body 2 page 15
Padding Shapes page 13
Applying Color page 18
Adding Fluffy Texture page 20
Making Basic Shapes: Legs and Tails page 9
Joining Basic Shapes page 11
Blending Joined Shapes page 12
Shaping Pieces page 13
Making Basic Shapes: Ears, Tails, and Wings page 10
Adding Ears page 21
Making an Eye page 20

1 Using white merino wool, make a Basic Body 2 (see page 15), making an egg-shaped body measuring 3¼in (8.5cm) long by 2in (5cm) wide at the fattest point. Make a head measuring 2½ x 1⅜in (6 x 3.5cm) from the same wool, making it an oval shape as shown below. Bring in all the loose fibers to shape and firm up the shape.

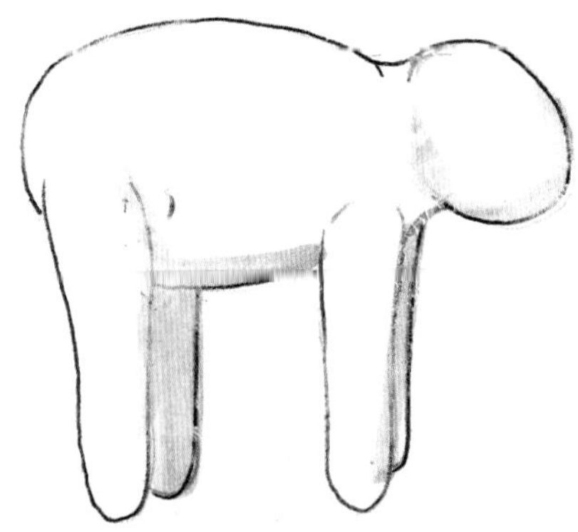

2 From four pieces of white merino wool make four legs (see page 9), each measuring 3in (8cm) long by ⅝in (1.5cm) wide. Attach the legs to the base of the body so that the legs are 1½in (4cm) long. Keep checking so that each finished leg is the same length.

3 Pull off some pieces of the carded sheep fleece and needle them over the whole body, legs, and head to quickly achieve a nice plump cub shape as shown (see page 13). The fleece is a bit too yellow and wooly for a polar bear cub, so cover it with a layer of long wefts of white merino wool (see page 18), working from the head backward. Try to keep it soft and furry (see page 20); the combination of the two wools gives a lovely texture.

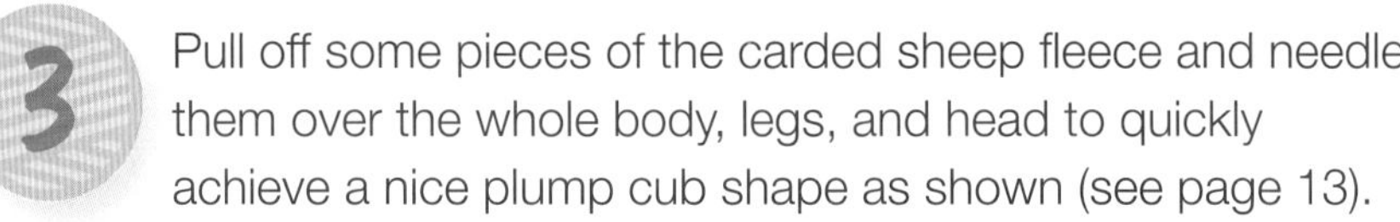

4 With white merino wool, create an oval sausage shape for the tail (see page 9), 1¼in (3cm) long. Attach it to the bear's rear end, as shown (see page 11), and blend in the join with a wisp of white merino wool (see page 12).

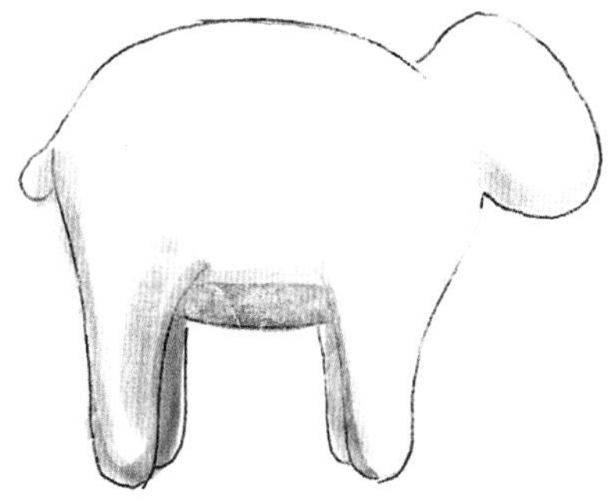

5 For the paws, bend over ¾in (2cm) of the ends of the legs, hold them with one hand and needle them into position (see page 13). Add three short wisps of black merino to define the toes (see page 19).

6 To create the muzzle, pinch the bridge of the nose with your fingers and then needle it into shape (see page 13). Add a few wisps of white merino to smooth the surface. Flatten the top of the head with the needle and shape the brow and the eye sockets.

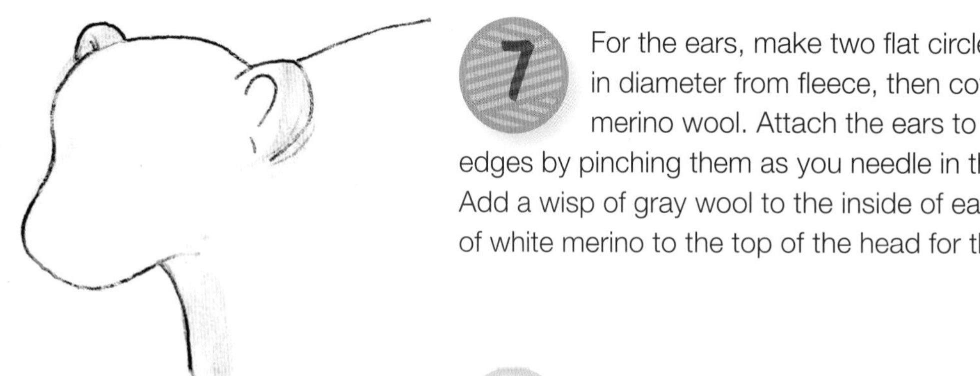

7 For the ears, make two flat circles (see page 10) 1in (2.5cm) in diameter from fleece, then cover both sides with white merino wool. Attach the ears to the head, curling in the edges by pinching them as you needle in the base (see page 21). Add a wisp of gray wool to the inside of each ear. Add a short wisp of white merino to the top of the head for the little cute quiff.

8 Add a wisp of gray carded wool to the end of the muzzle (see page 18). Use black wool to make an upside-down triangle for the nose. Use a sliver of gray wool to make the mouth; start by needling on the middle of the strand just under the nose and then guide the ends into place with the needle.

9 Add a small amount of black wool to the eye sockets for the eyes, then add a tiny spot of white wool for the highlight. Add short wisps of white merino wool to the top of the eyes for the eyelids (see page 20).

Handsome Zebra

           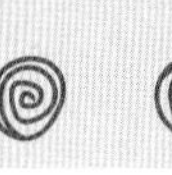   

Zebra stripes are unique, so you can be as inventive as you like when adding patterns of lines and curves to your felted animal. Zebras are related to horses and donkeys and live on the plains of Africa, where they escape predators by running from side to side.

You will need

Merino wool in
white 1oz (30g)
black 0.7oz (20g)

Carded wool in mottled gray 0.18oz (5g)

Felting needle with handle

Foam block

Sharp embroidery scissors

Techniques Checklist

Basic Body 1 page 14
Blending Joined Shapes page 12
Padding Shapes page 13
Shaping Pieces page 13
Making Basic Shapes: Ears, Tails, and Wings page 10
Applying Color page 18
Adding Ears page 21
Extending Shapes page 13
Making Basic Shapes: Legs and Tails page 9
Adding Fluffy Texture page 20
Joining Basic Shapes page 11
Making an Eye page 20

1 Use white wool and follow Basic Body 1 (see page 14), to make an egg-shaped body measuring 4in (10cm) long by 2in (5.5cm) wide at the fattest point. From the same wool, make the neck 3¼in (8.5cm) long and 1¼in (3cm) wide at the base. Make and attach white wool legs, making them 3½in (9cm) long and ¾in (2cm) wide. Attach them with 2⅞in (7.5cm) of leg hanging down below the body, making sure that they are level.

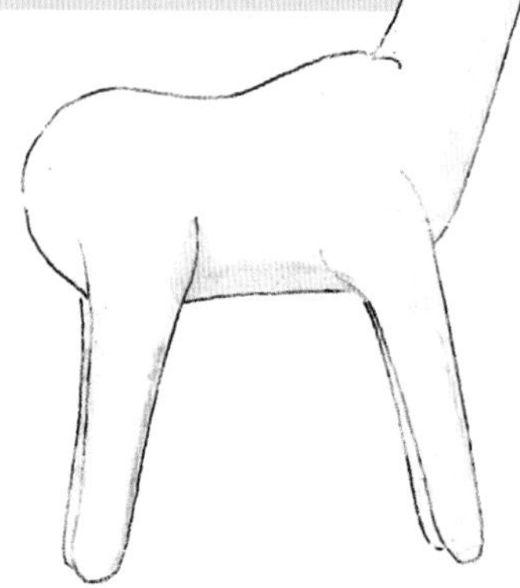

2 Wrap a weft of wool around the top of each leg, needling on the loose ends over the haunch to help secure the join and build up the shape (see page 12). Build up the back haunches with a few curled wisps of white wool (see page 13), then squeeze and needle all four legs until they are slender (see page 13). Smooth out the protruding chest with a few folded wefts at the base of the neck, then needle in the curve at the back of the neck. Squeeze in the sides of the body between the legs and under the belly and needle them, then squeeze down the dip in the back and needle that.

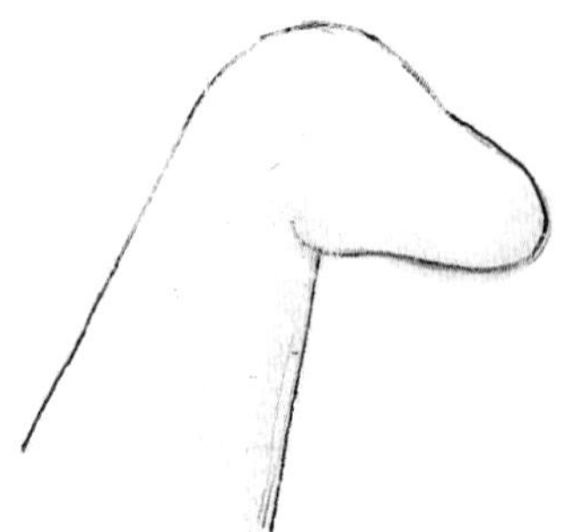

3 For the head, make an egg shape measuring 2⅝ x 1¾in (6.5 x 4.5cm) with the white wool and follow Basic Body 1 to attach it to the top of the neck at the angle shown. Shape the head to create the muzzle, jaw, brow, and top of the head by using your fingers to pinch and squeeze while needling the wool.

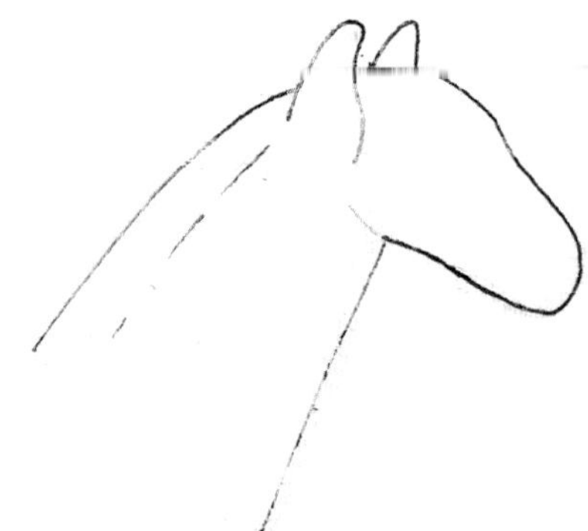

4 For the ears, use white wool to make two flat, teardrop shapes (see page 10) measuring 1⅜ x ¾in (3.5 x 2cm). Shade the insides with gray carded wool (see page 18). Attach the ears to the sides of the head, shaping the ears by squeezing them inward (see page 21). Add a wisp of white on the back to blend in the join. Add a few folded wefts to the back of the neck to create the mane ridge, needling the fold onto the center line and smoothing the ends over the neck (see page 13). Lay wefts of white wool over the neck to smooth the surface.

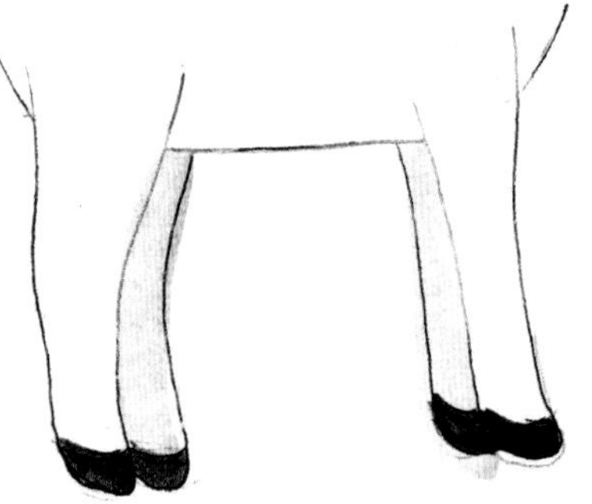

5 Move the legs into position—either standing straight or slightly bent for walking. Needle the tops to hold them in place. Extend the legs by ¾in (2cm) with a few wisps of gray carded wool wrapped around the ends (see page 13). Needle in the top of the gray wool to shape the ankles, then shape the hooves by needling the bottom flat and working the needle into the back to angle it. Wrap wisps of white wool over the lower legs, so that only the shaped hooves are left gray.

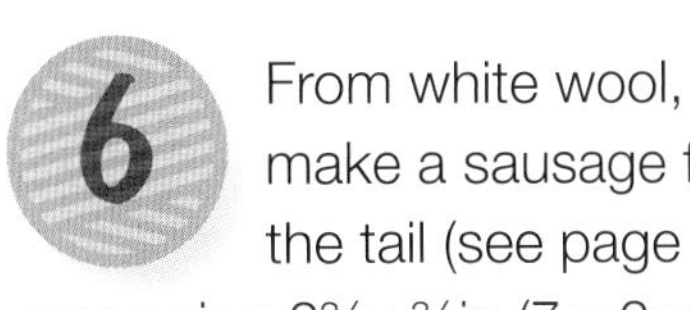

6 From white wool, make a sausage for the tail (see page 9) measuring 2¾x ¾in (7 x 2cm), leaving loose fibers at one end. Roll and needle the other end to make it slimmer, then needle on one end of a black wisp (see page 20).

7 Roll a few strands of black wool between your fingers to make a thin strip. Needle a length of black strip around the tail, then cut it with the scissors and needle it smooth; do not indent the stripes into the tail (see page 19). Do the same again to cover the tail with stripes. Attach the tail and blend it in with a wisp of white wool (see page 11).

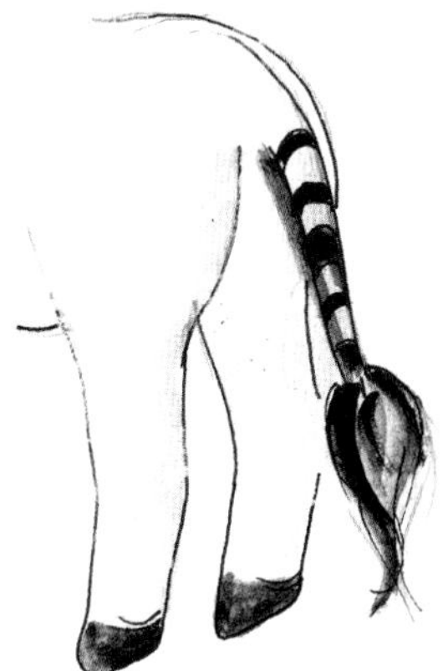

8 Wrap a few wisps of black wool around the end of the muzzle to make it longer and create the long lip (see page 13). Needle in the dips for the eye sockets, then fill them with pea-sized almonds of black wool (see page 20). Add a thin line of black above the eye for the eye lashes. Cover the body with black stripes in the same way as for the tail, using a variety of thicknesses and lengths of black stripes.

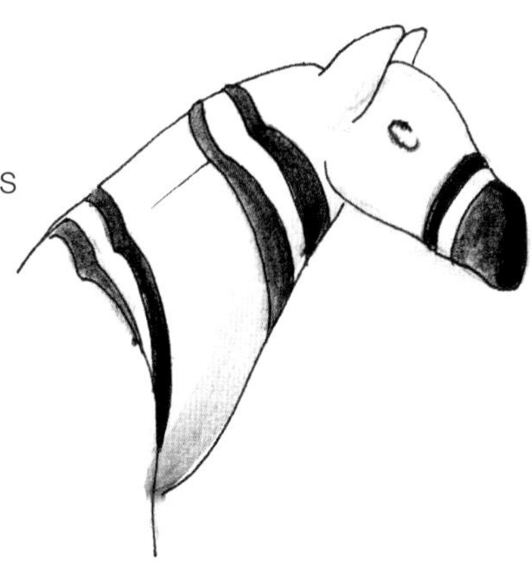

9 When all the stripes are done, add a few short wisps of black wool between the ears and running about ¾in (2cm) down the neck for the mane (see page 20). Then add a narrow band of gray just above the muzzle and a thin line of gray for the mouth. Use very thin strips of white wool to make tiny ovals for the nostrils.

Panda Power

With a cuddly soft tummy and bendable arms, this lovable panda is great fun to make, using just two colors of wool and some easy shaping. Did you know, Giant Pandas live high in the mountains in China and spend 12 hours a day eating?

You will need

Merino wool in
white 0.7oz (20g)
black 1oz (30g)

Felting needle with handle

Foam block

Metal skewer

Two chenille stems (pipe cleaners)

Sharp embroidery scissors

Techniques Checklist

Making Basic Shapes: Bodies and Heads page 8
Joining Basic Shapes page 11
Blending Joined Shapes page 12
Needling Wool around a Skewer page 18
Padding Shapes page 13
Shaping Pieces page 13
Making Basic Shapes: Ears, Tails, and Wings page 10
Adding Ears page 21
Making an Eye page 20
Applying Color page 18

1 Take a generous weft of white wool, curl it into a roll, and make an egg-shaped body measuring 3½in (9cm) long by 2¾in (7cm) wide at the fattest point, using the needle to push in the ends toward the middle. With a smaller weft of white wool, make an egg-shaped head measuring 2 x 1½in (5 x 4cm). Bring in all the loose fibers to shape and firm up the egg (see page 8).

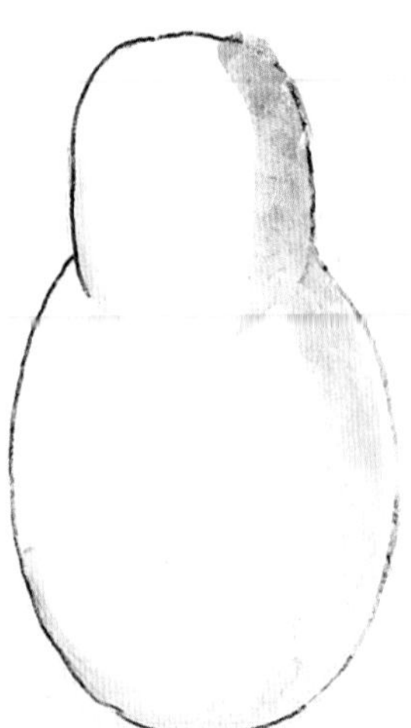

2 To join the head to the top of the body, hold the pieces in position and wrap a weft of white wool around the neck, like a scarf, and needle it on to blend the head and body together (see page 11), pushing the needle through one edge of the smaller egg into the other egg and taking it out so the fibers fuse. Blend the pieces all around the edge (see page 12).

3 To make the front and the back legs, wrap a long weft of black wool around a skewer, place it on a foam pad, and needle it all over to create a tube 8¼in (21cm) long. Make two needled tubes, one for the front legs and one for the back (see page 18).

Is it LUNCHTIME yet?

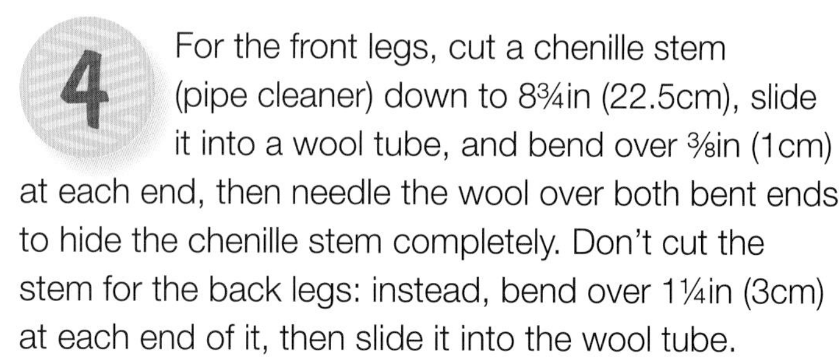

4 For the front legs, cut a chenille stem (pipe cleaner) down to 8¾in (22.5cm), slide it into a wool tube, and bend over ⅜in (1cm) at each end, then needle the wool over both bent ends to hide the chenille stem completely. Don't cut the stem for the back legs: instead, bend over 1¼in (3cm) at each end of it, then slide it into the wool tube. Cover the ends.

5 To join the legs to the body, hold the middle of the front legs in position just below the back of the head, then wrap a weft of black wool over the legs and around the neck, as shown. Needle the weft on to hold the legs in place, taking the needle from the body into the legs to fuse the fibers (see page 12).

6 Hold the back legs at the back of the base of the body, wrap a weft of black wool around the bottom of the body, and needle it on to hold the legs in place. Add more wool if needed and needle the body to make the joins over the legs smooth. Curve the arms and legs around, so that the panda can sit upright.

7 Now you can start to shape your panda by padding it out. Wrap a weft of black wool around the top of each back leg and needle it on to fill out the hips (see page 13). Then take a big weft of white wool and needle it over the panda's bottom, a bit like a diaper, so that just the black legs are visible. Add more wefts of black wool to the front and back legs and thighs, and white wool to the tummy to make the body chunkier.

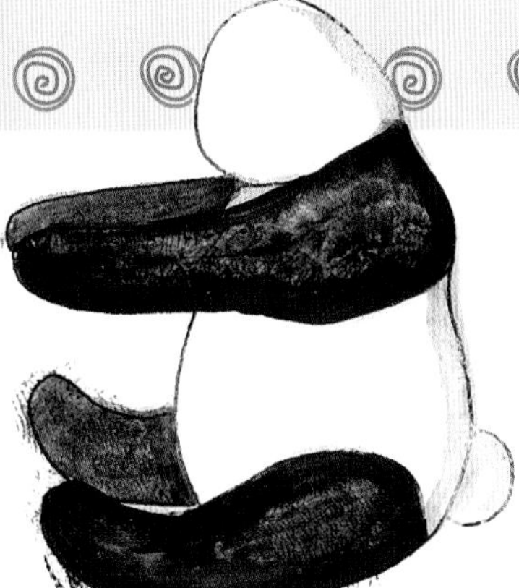

8 Bend over the tips of the legs for the paws and needle in all around the ankles to shape the pieces, pinching and squeezing to give a defined shape (see page 13). Make a small ball of white wool and attach it to the base of the back for a fluffy tail (see page 11).

9 To shape the head, needle a folded weft or pillow of white wool to the back of the neck, overlapping the top of the black stripe on the back (see page 13). Build it up so that there is a smooth curve from the back to the top of the head. For the ears, make two flat circles 1¼in (3cm) in diameter (see page 21). Attach the ears toward the back of the head, needling on the base of each ear in a curve and curling the whole shape inward while needling (see page 21).

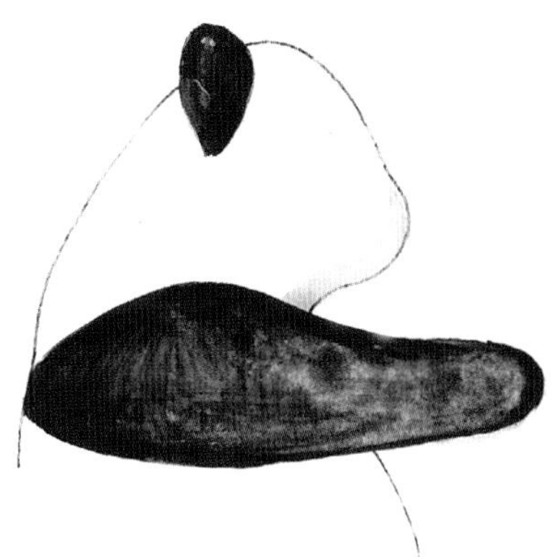

10 Curl a wisp of white wool into a pillow shape and add it to the front of the head to start shaping the muzzle (see page 13). Add a few folded wisps of white to pad out the cheeks, placing the folded end of each wisp where the muzzle joins the head to build up the shape. Needle in the dips for the eye sockets to the side of the top of the muzzle (see page 13). Needle a pea-sized ball of black wool into each socket, positioning them to create the slightly angled eye patches.

11 Add a small piece of white wool for the white of each eye, then add a very small bit of black for the pupil (see page 20). Needle on a small oval of black for the nose, then add a sliver of black for the mouth; start by needling on the middle of the strand just under the nose, and then guide the ends into place with the needle (see page 19).

Lord Lion

Fierce and proud, a lion is an impressive beast with a truly magnificent hairstyle! You can make your lion stand, run, sit, or lie down by shaping the body in different positions. Have fun creating his mane from fluffy wool, or make it without the mane to create a lady lioness.

You will need

Merino wool in
banana-yellow 1oz (30g)
dark brown 0.07oz (2g)
white 0.18oz (5g)
light brown 0.07oz (2g)
black 0.18oz (5g)
orange 0.03oz (1g)
green 0.03oz (1g)

Curly doll hair in
golden-yellow 0.18oz (5g)

Felting needle with handle

Foam block

Sharp embroidery scissors

Techniques Checklist

Basic Body 2 page 15
Blending Joined Shapes page 12
Padding Shapes page 13
Shaping Pieces page 13
Applying Color page 18
Making Basic Shapes: Legs and Tails page 9
Extending Shapes page 13
Making Basic Shapes: Ears, Tails, and Wings page 10
Making an Eye page 20
Adding Fluffy Texture page 20

KING of the JUNGLE!

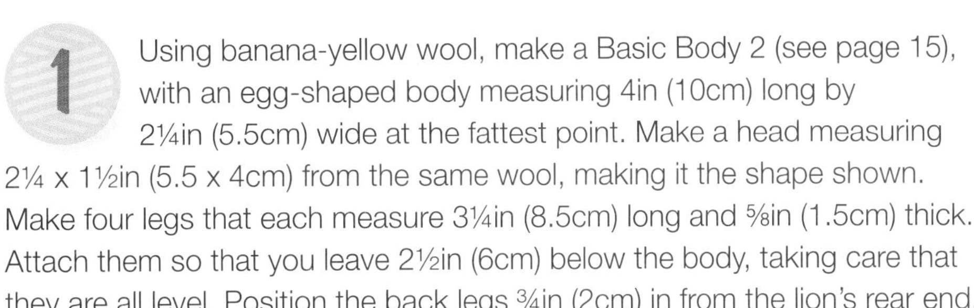

1 Using banana-yellow wool, make a Basic Body 2 (see page 15), with an egg-shaped body measuring 4in (10cm) long by 2¼in (5.5cm) wide at the fattest point. Make a head measuring 2¼ x 1½in (5.5 x 4cm) from the same wool, making it the shape shown. Make four legs that each measure 3¼in (8.5cm) long and ⅝in (1.5cm) thick. Attach them so that you leave 2½in (6cm) below the body, taking care that they are all level. Position the back legs ¾in (2cm) in from the lion's rear end.

2 Wrap a weft of banana-yellow wool around the very top of each leg, with the loose ends going over the back of the lion, and needle this lightly to blend the leg into the body and create a hip (see page 12). Add folded yellow wisps to the top of each leg, attaching the folded side to the center line on the back and needling the fibers down the leg to build up the neck and shoulders and the curve on the rear end (see page 13).

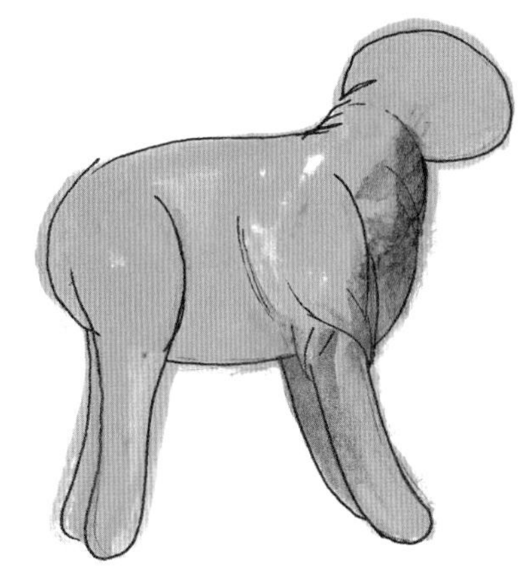

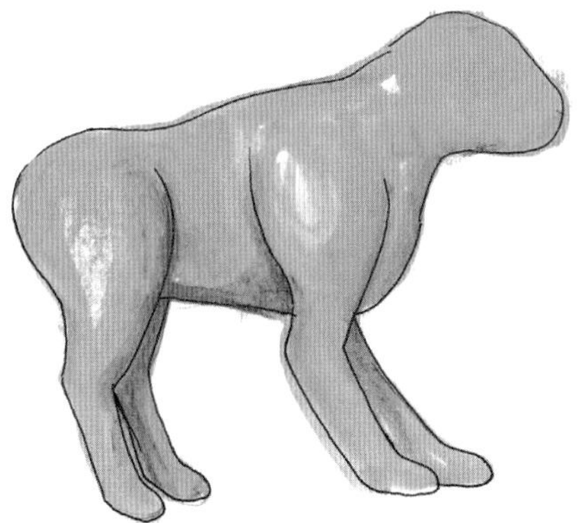

3 Create the contours on the body by needling and pinching (see page 13). Holding the body in one hand, needle in between the back legs to make the curve of the rib cage and tummy. Next, work the needle on the sides of the rib cage between the front and back legs to shape the flanks and haunches. Pinch in the lion's sides and needle down the back to bring out the curve of the spine.

TIP

If you would like your lion to sit down, fold the back legs in half and needle them into a right-angled shape before attaching to the body.

4 To create the paws, bend ¾in (2cm) of the ends of the front legs and ⅜in (1cm) of the back legs at right angles, and needle into place. Pinch and needle the legs to shape them, as shown. Add a few strands of dark brown wool to each paw to define the toes (see page 19).

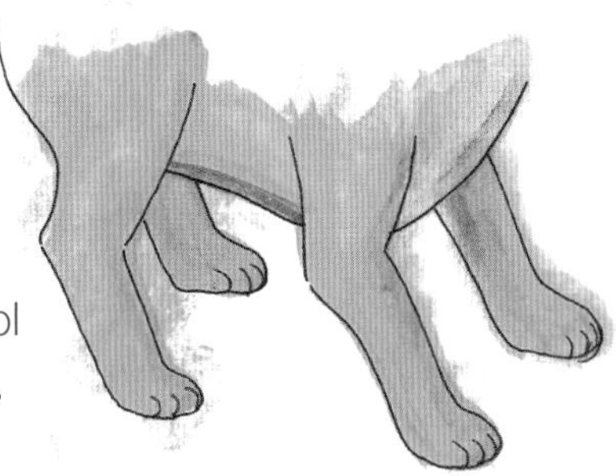

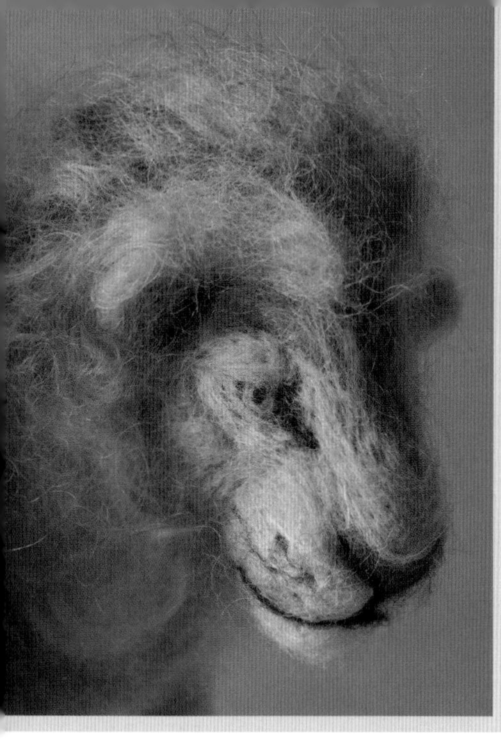

5 For the tail, make a slim sausage 2¾in (7.5cm) long in banana-yellow wool (see page 9), leaving loose fibers at both ends. Attach one end to the base of the back.

6 Pinch and needle the sides of the narrow end of the head to create the muzzle and curved profile (see page 13). Extend the muzzle and chin with a wisp of banana-yellow wool and add more wisps to the top of the muzzle to build up the shape (see page 18). Define the eyes by needling in the eye sockets.

7 With the banana-yellow wool, create two ears from flat almond shapes, 1¼in (3cm) long (see page 10). Attach them to the head just behind the eye sockets, pointing slightly outward. Shade the inside of the ears with wisps of white and light brown wool and add wisps of white wool to the chin and cheeks (see page 19).

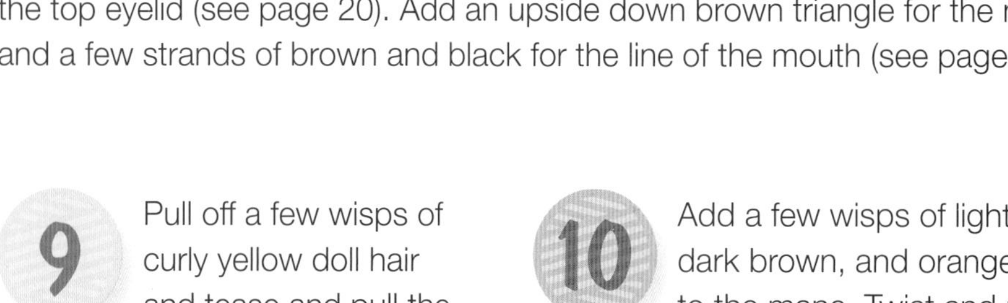

8 Add dark brown to the eye sockets in an almond shape, with a strand pointing down toward the mouth. Define the eye shape with a white outline and add a green iris and black pupil, with a wisp of yellow for the top eyelid (see page 20). Add an upside down brown triangle for the nose and a few strands of brown and black for the line of the mouth (see page 19).

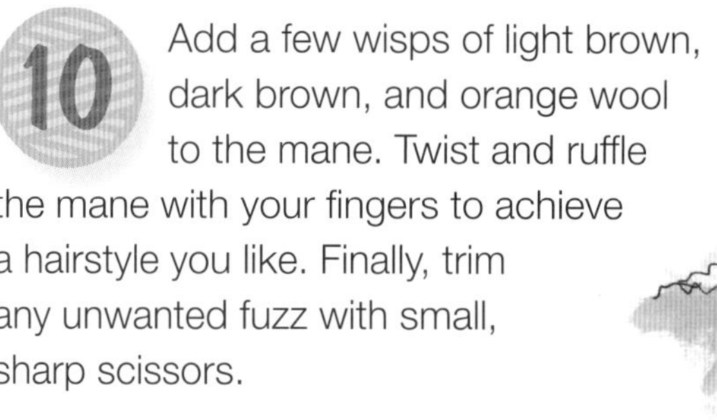

9 Pull off a few wisps of curly yellow doll hair and tease and pull the fibers apart to make some fluffy texture. Needle on small pieces, building up the mane gradually (see page 20).

10 Add a few wisps of light brown, dark brown, and orange wool to the mane. Twist and ruffle the mane with your fingers to achieve a hairstyle you like. Finally, trim any unwanted fuzz with small, sharp scissors.

Cute Cub

There's lots of coloring and pattern-making to keep you busy in this project—tiny dots and ringed stripes will make your cub come alive. A cheetah cub's fur is known as a mantle, and is really thick when it is born to help to protect it from predators.

You will need

Merino wool in
white 0.7oz (20g)
charcoal black 0.10oz (3g)
golden yellow 0.18oz (5g)
dark brown 0.03oz (1g)

Alpaca wool in
mottled beige 0.35oz (10g)
fawn 0.07oz (2g)
white 0.18oz (5g)

Felting needle with handle

Foam block

Sharp embroidery scissors

Techniques Checklist

Basic Body 2 page 15
Shaping Pieces page 13
Padding Shapes page 13
Extending Shapes page 13
Making Basic Shapes: Legs and Tails page 9
Joining Basic Shapes page 11
Blending Joined Shapes page 12
Adding Fluffy Texture page 20
Applying Color page 18
Making Basic Shapes: Ears, Tails, and Wings page 10
Adding Ears page 21
Making an Eye page 20

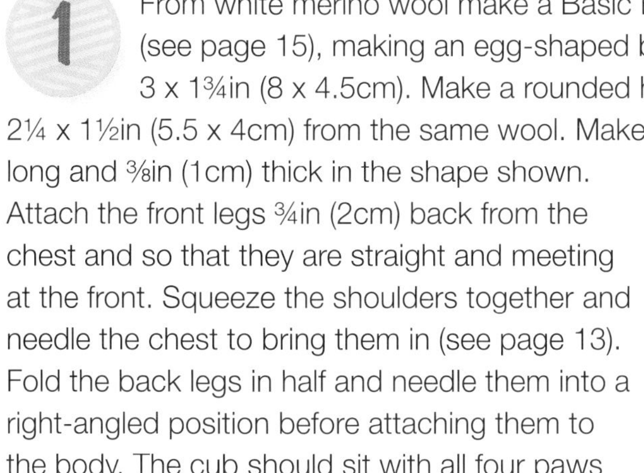

1 From white merino wool make a Basic Body 2 (see page 15), making an egg-shaped body measuring 3 x 1¾in (8 x 4.5cm). Make a rounded head measuring 2¼ x 1½in (5.5 x 4cm) from the same wool. Make the legs 3in (8cm) long and ⅜in (1cm) thick in the shape shown. Attach the front legs ¾in (2cm) back from the chest and so that they are straight and meeting at the front. Squeeze the shoulders together and needle the chest to bring them in (see page 13). Fold the back legs in half and needle them into a right-angled position before attaching them to the body. The cub should sit with all four paws on the ground.

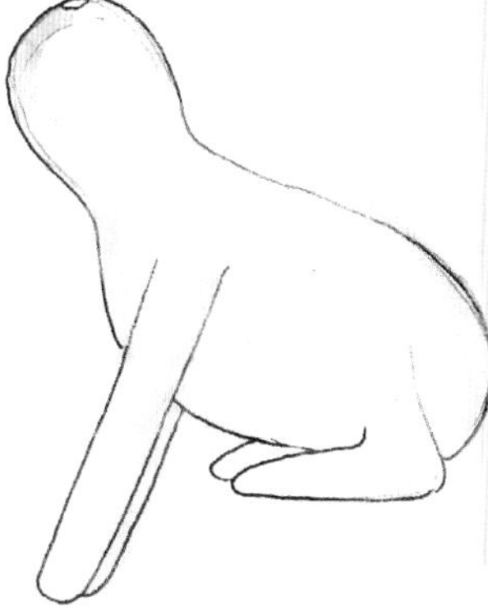

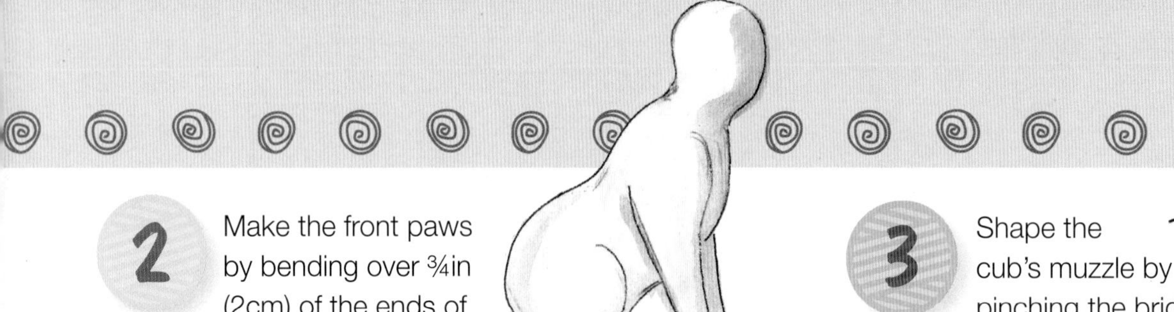

2 Make the front paws by bending over ¾in (2cm) of the ends of the legs and needling them into position (see page 13). Squeeze the back end together and needle the curve of the back and tucked-in tummy. Add folded wefts of white wool over the back to smooth the joins with the legs, positioning the fold at the back of the neck (see page 13). Wrap a weft of white wool around the neck like a scarf, to pad out the curve. Pad out the shoulders and haunches by adding curled wefts of white wool.

3 Shape the cub's muzzle by pinching the bridge of the nose and needling it, then wrap a wisp of white wool over the muzzle to make it longer (see page 13). A cheetah cub's head is quite large in relation to its body, so pad out the head with folded wefts of white wool across the top and back of the head. Pad out the cheeks by needling on curled wisps of white wool.

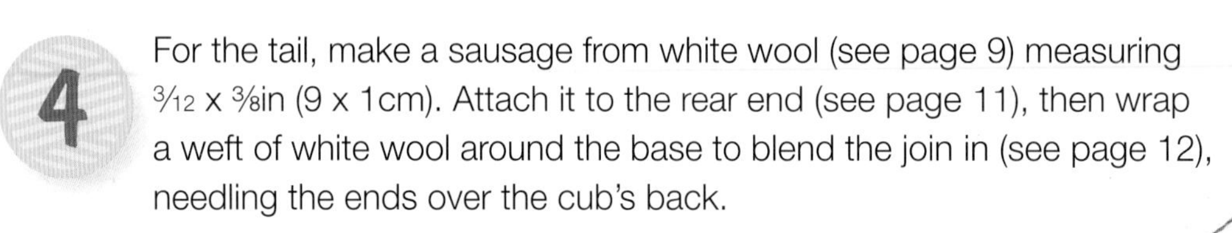

4 For the tail, make a sausage from white wool (see page 9) measuring 3½ x ⅜in (9 x 1cm). Attach it to the rear end (see page 11), then wrap a weft of white wool around the base to blend the join in (see page 12), needling the ends over the cub's back.

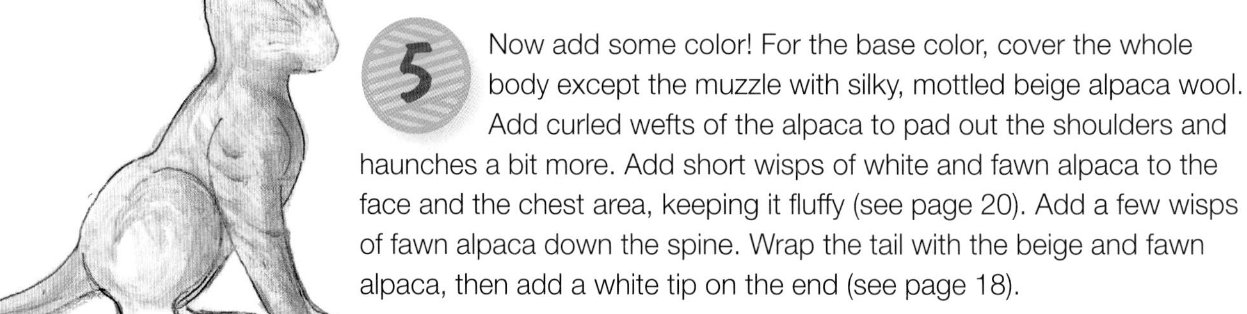

5 Now add some color! For the base color, cover the whole body except the muzzle with silky, mottled beige alpaca wool. Add curled wefts of the alpaca to pad out the shoulders and haunches a bit more. Add short wisps of white and fawn alpaca to the face and the chest area, keeping it fluffy (see page 20). Add a few wisps of fawn alpaca down the spine. Wrap the tail with the beige and fawn alpaca, then add a white tip on the end (see page 18).

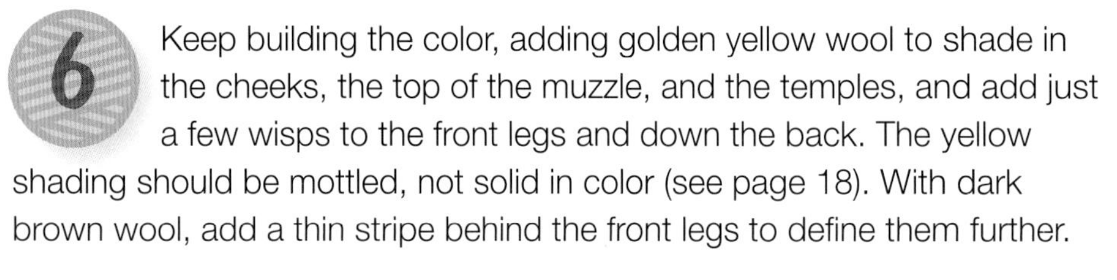

6 Keep building the color, adding golden yellow wool to shade in the cheeks, the top of the muzzle, and the temples, and add just a few wisps to the front legs and down the back. The yellow shading should be mottled, not solid in color (see page 18). With dark brown wool, add a thin stripe behind the front legs to define them further.

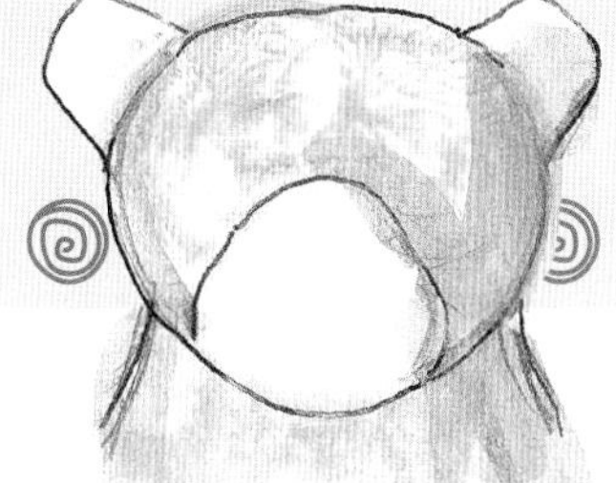

From white wool, make two flat almond shapes for ears (see page 10) measuring ⅝ x 1in (1.5 x 2.5cm). Attach them to the head at the angle shown (see page 21), taking care to keep them level. Add a bit of fawn alpaca to blend the back of the ears into the head, and curve the tips with the needle.

8

For the face, needle in the eye sockets, then add a small pea-sized amount of black wool in an almond shape for the eyes. Add a strip of black wool for the long mark starting from the corner of each eye, running down the side of the muzzle, then under the chin (see page 18). Make the irises with a bit of golden-yellow wool, then add a dot of black wool for the pupil (see page 20).

9

Outline the eyes with a strip of white merino wool, then add a thin, short strip of dark brown, starting at the outer edge of the eye and running to the bottom of the ears. Add a heart shape of black wool for the nose, then add a sliver of black wool for the mouth; start by needling on the middle of the strand just under the nose, then guide the ends into place with the needle. Use beige alpaca to add three stripes on the brow, running from between the eyes over the top of the head. Start with the center stripe then add the outer stripes, to keep it balanced.

10

Add small spots of black wool in different sizes over the whole body, using different amounts of wool (see page 19). You can always add more wool if the spot disappears after needling. Wrap a long strip of black wool in a spiral around the tail and needle it on, then needle a wisp of black wool to the tip of the tail.

11

Add just a small amount of fawn alpaca over the stripes to soften them a little. Curl the tail into position so that it is wrapped around the body, as you needle the wool on. Add a few short strips of dark brown wool to the paws to define the toes.

Orang-Utan Baby

You will need

Carded wool in
mottled dark gray 0.70oz (20g)

Merino wool in
peach 0.35oz (10g)
black 0.07oz (2g)
white 0.07oz (2g)
brown 0.35oz (10g)
orange 0.03oz (1g)

Two chenille stems (pipe cleaners)

Metal skewer

Felting needle with handle

Foam block

Sharp embroidery scissors

Techniques Checklist

Needling Wool around a Skewer page 18
Making Basic Shapes: Bodies and Heads page 8
Joining Basic Shapes page 11
Blending Joined Shapes page 12
Making Basic Shapes: Ears, Tails, and Wings page 10
Shaping Pieces page 13
Applying Color page 18
Padding Shapes page 13
Making an Eye page 20
Adding Ears page 21
Adding Fluffy Texture page 20

Definitely top of the cuteness scale, Orang-utan babies have crazy hair and adorable eyes. This project uses chenille stems so that you can bend the arms and legs into any pose you like. Orang-utans are an endangered species—do what you can to raise awareness to help protect them.

1 To make the arms and legs, wrap a long weft of carded gray wool around a skewer, place it on a foam block, and needle it all over to create a tube 8¼in (21cm) long. Make two needled tubes (see page 18). Cut the chenille stems (pipe cleaners) down to 8¾in (22.5cm), slide each into a wool tube, and bend over ⅜in (1cm) at each end, then needle the wool over both bent ends to hide the chenille stem completely.

2 Make an egg shape measuring 1½in (4cm) long by 2½in (6cm) wide at the fattest point (see page 8) from gray carded wool, using the needle to push in the ends toward the middle. The narrow end will be the top and the fat end the base of the body. One covered chenille stem makes both arms. Position one covered stem centrally on the front of the body, ⅜in (1cm) down from the top, and attach it with a weft of gray wool over the central section, needling it firmly in place to secure the arms to the body.

Just hanging around!

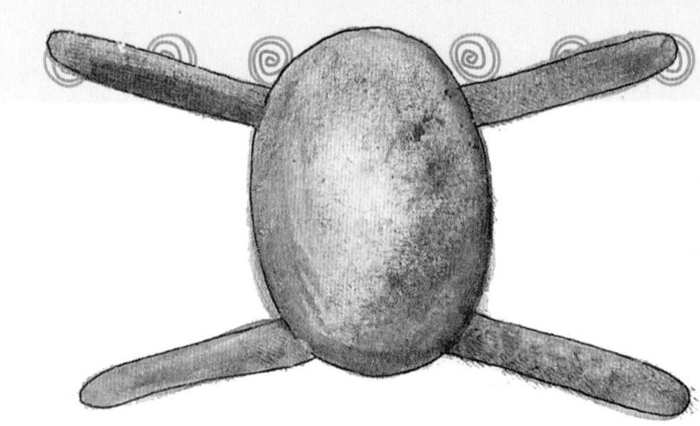

3 For the legs, attach the other chenille stem in the same way, ⅜in (1cm) up from the base of the body. Add more wool if needed and needle the body to make the joins over the legs and arms smooth. Bend the chenille stems so that the body can sit upright, balanced on the legs.

4 From gray carded wool, make a small egg shape measuring 1½ x 1¼in (4 x 3cm) for the head and attach it to the top of the body (see page 11). Then add a few wisps of gray wool around the neck to blend the head into the shoulders (see page 12).

5 Use peach wool to make a flat oval (see page 10) measuring 1 x ⅜in (2.5 x 1cm); this will be a hand. Leave loose fibers at one end. Make a sausage measuring ⅜ x ¼in (1 x 0.5cm) for the thumb and attach it to make a mitten shape (see page 11). Curl the mitten and needle it to create a curled hand (see page 13). Make two hands, then make two feet that are the same as the hands, but slightly longer, about 1¼ x ⅜in (3 x 1cm). Add strands of gray wool to each piece to define fingers and toes (see page 19).

6 Attach the hands and feet to the ends of the arms and legs, making sure that the thumbs and big toes are positioned on the inside. Wrap a bit of peach wool around the wrist and ankle to secure the hands and feet, then use a little gray wool to cover up any peach that has strayed onto the arms and legs.

7 Build up the neck and blend the head smoothly into the shoulders (see page 13). For the mouth, make a half-egg of peach wool measuring 1 x ¾in (2.5 x 2cm) and needle to the front of the head, as shown, needling around the base so that the piece is firmly attached and well defined (see page 11). Needle on two pea-sized discs of peach wool for the eye sockets.

8 Add a wisp of black wool in each peach eye socket for the eyes, then add white highlights (see page 20). Needle on a pea-sized ball of brown wool for the nose and a thin strand of brown wool for the line of the mouth (see page 19).

9 Needle two pea-sized pieces of peach wool into flat oval shapes for the ears (see page 10). Attach one to each side of the head, as shown, curling them with your fingers as you do so (see page 21).

10 Add wisps of brown wool all over the body and back of the head. Keep them soft and fluffy by not overworking them with the needle (see page 20). Add short fluffy wisps of orange to the top of the head and the chest. Orang-utan babies often have crazy hair—make a quiff or mohawk if you like!

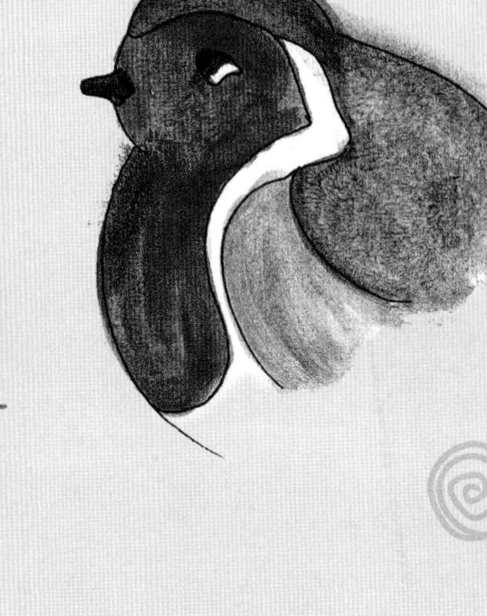

chapter 2

Feathered Friends

Teeny Tiny Penguin

Baby penguin chicks are covered in a coat of soft, fluffy down, which is perfect to recreate with felting! This little chick is an Emperor Penguin, and his black-and-white face markings make him stand out against the snow.

You will need

Carded wool in
mottled dark gray 0.18oz (5g)
mottled light gray 0.03oz (1g)

Merino wool in
black 0.18oz (5g)
white 0.10oz (3g)
peach 0.01oz (0.5g)

Felting needle with handle

Foam block

Sharp embroidery scissors

Techniques Checklist

Making Basic Shapes: Bodies and Heads page 8
Applying Color page 18
Joining Basic Shapes page 11
Blending Joined Shapes page 12
Adding Fluffy Texture page 20
Padding Shapes page 13
Making Basic Shapes: Necks and Beaks page 10
Making Basic Shapes: Ears, Tails, and Wings page 10

1 Start by making an egg-shaped body (see page 8) measuring 2½ x 1½in (6 x 4cm) in dark gray wool. The narrow end will be the top and the fat end the base of the body. Make two flat, oval shapes measuring 2 x 1in (5 x 2.5cm) from the same wool for the wings. Shade one side of each wing in white (see page 18).

2 Attach the wings to the sides of the body, white sides facing in and starting about ⅜in (1cm) down from the top. Only attach ⅜in (1cm) of the top of each wing, leaving the rest loose (see page 11). Put a wisp of gray wool over each join to secure the wing and build the shape up (see page 12). Turn the body in all directions to check that the wings are level. Add some light gray wool to build up the body and make it round and fluffy (see page 20).

3 Fold a large weft of black wool in half and lay it on the top of the body, folded side at the front. Needle the fold to the body to define the lower edge of the head (see page 13). Turn the body around and needle in the loose fibers, so that the back of the head blends smoothly into the back of the body. Needle the whole head lightly into shape. Add further wisps of black wool, keeping the head shape correct, until the head is the right size. Then cover the back of the head in dark gray wool, leaving just the face black.

4 Bring the dark gray on the head forward in a point onto the forehead—this is called a 'widow's peak.' Add a small wisp of white wool to give it a fluffy texture (see page 20). Add a pea-sized piece of white wool to the cheeks on both sides, then join them with a few strands of white under the chin to create a "U" shape (see page 18). Add a tiny black dot for each eye, as shown. Then add a few wisps of white wool to the chest.

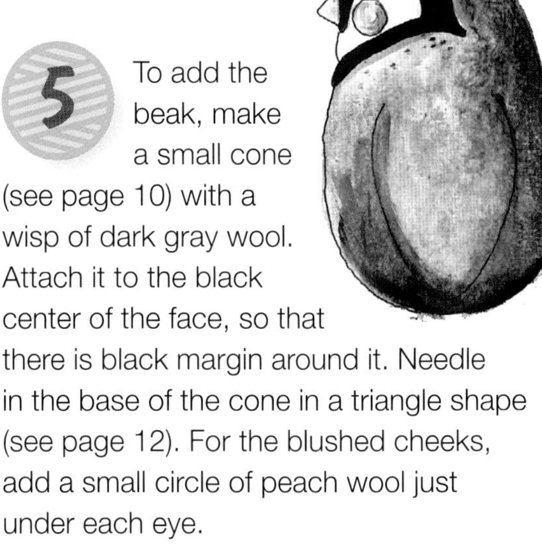

5 To add the beak, make a small cone (see page 10) with a wisp of dark gray wool. Attach it to the black center of the face, so that there is black margin around it. Needle in the base of the cone in a triangle shape (see page 12). For the blushed cheeks, add a small circle of peach wool just under each eye.

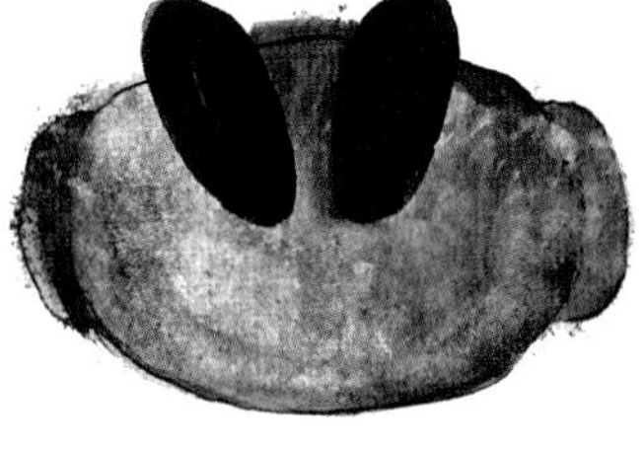

6 For the feet, make two flat, teardrop shapes measuring 1¼in (3cm) long (see page 10). Attach them to the base of the body with the wider end sticking out at the front, as shown. Needle on a piece of gray wool over the narrow end to hold the feet firmly in place.

ANTARCTIC antics!

Red Robin

Robins are known as the gardener's companion, following you around to catch any tasty worms that appear as you dig! Their bright and cheery colors make them look very festive—why not make several to use as Christmas decorations?

You will need

Merino wool in
light gray 0.18oz (5g)
dark brown 0.10oz (3g)
dark gray 0.07oz (2g)
white 0.03oz (1g)
red 0.07oz (2g)
orange/pink 0.01oz (0.5g)
black 0.01oz (0.5g)

Felting needle with handle

Polystyrene ball 1½in (4cm) in diameter

Foam block

Sharp embroidery scissors

Techniques Checklist

Applying Color page 18
Making Basic Shapes: Bodies and Heads page 8
Basic Body 3 page 16
Adding Fluffy Texture page 20
Making Basic Shapes: Necks and Beaks page 10
Joining Basic Shapes page 11
Padding Shapes page 13
Making an Eye page 20

1 Pull off a weft of light gray wool and wrap it over the ball. Hold it in place with one hand and jab the needle repeatedly all over the surface with the other hand. Needle on more wool until the whole ball is covered. Roll it in your hands to smooth in any loose fibers. Add a layer of dark brown (see page 18) in the shape shown for the body. Add a small ball (see page 8) of dark brown for the head. Follow Basic Body 3 (see page 16) to make a tail in dark brown.

2 Make two wings from dark gray wool, following Basic Body 3 (see page 16), making them the shape shown. Needle a layer of white wool onto the chest, taking it down under the tummy; needle it quite lightly so that it is a bit fluffy (see page 20).

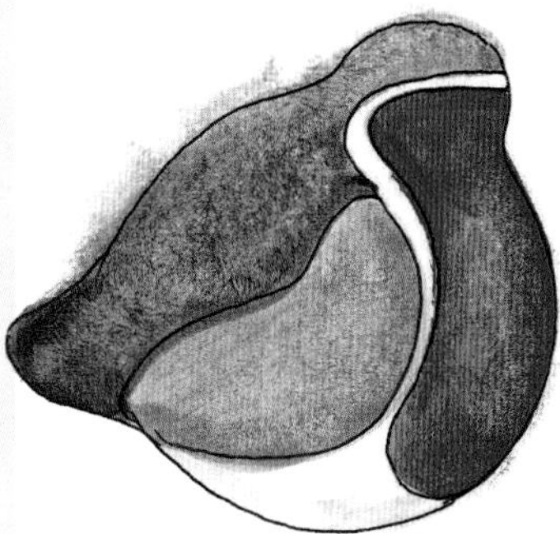

3 Now add a layer of red wool to the chest and face. Build up the chest with wisps of wool so that the red is solid, with no pale gray showing through, then add a small wisp of pink or orange to give some texture (see page 18). Outline the face with a narrow stripe of white wool.

Little Robin REDBREAST

4 Make a tiny cone of black wool on the foam block (see page 10) and attach it to the front of the head (see page 11). Shape a small ball of red wool into an oval with your fingers, then needle it on below the beak to shape the face (see page 13).

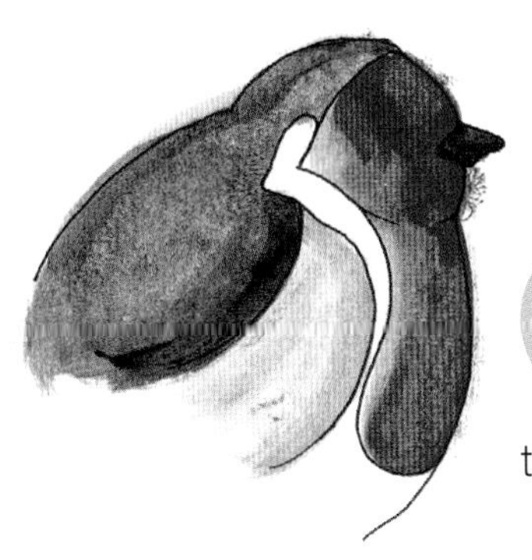

5 Lay a small weft of red wool over the face above the beak, wrapping it down onto the padded chin. Needle this on (see page 18), then needle in the chin line to help to define the round face and puffed-out chest.

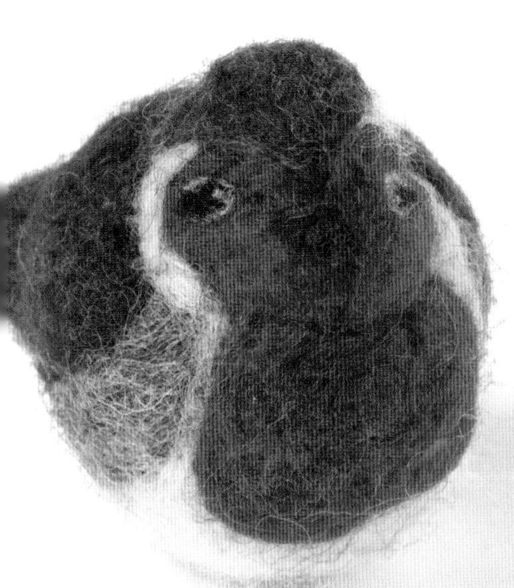

6 Add small almonds of white wool to each side of the head for the eyes, checking that they are level when viewed from the front, then add black pupils and white highlights (see page 20). Add a little brown wool to the top of the head to make the pointed shape between the eyes (known as a widow's peak).

SAFETY NOTE

Since the robin has a polystyrene ball in its core, it is not safe for children under 3 years old to play with.

Cheerful Chicken

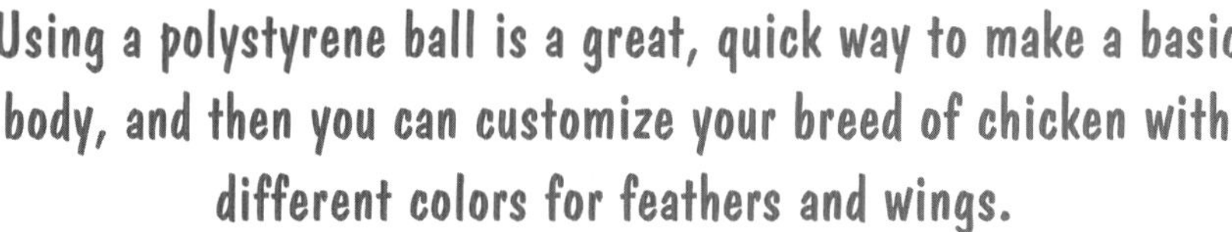

Using a polystyrene ball is a great, quick way to make a basic body, and then you can customize your breed of chicken with different colors for feathers and wings.

You will need

Merino wool in
white 0.18oz (5g)
red 0.07oz (2g)
light gray 0.18oz (5g)
light orange/yellow 0.07oz (2g)
black 0.01oz (0.5g)
dark gray 0.07oz (2g)

Polystyrene ball 1½in (4cm) in diameter

Felting needle with handle

Foam block

Sharp embroidery scissors

Techniques Checklist

Making Basic Shapes: Bodies and Heads page 8
Applying Color page 18
Padding Shapes page 13
Shaping Pieces page 13
Basic Body 3 page 16
Adding Fluffy Texture page 20
Making Basic Shapes: Necks and Beaks page 10

1 Pull off a weft of white wool and wrap it over the ball. Hold it in place with one ha[nd] and jab the needle all over the surface. N[eedle] on more wool until the whole ball is covered and sn[ug]. Roll it in your hands to smooth in any loose fibers. [A]… a small ball (see page 8) of white for the head, mak[ing] it the shape shown below.

2 Fold a wisp of red wool into a strip and attach one end to the center of the forehead, then needle the strip on in a straight line to the back of the head (see page 18). Don't flatten it by over-felting: it just needs to be firmly attached. Add some more red wool strips on top of the first to build the shape (see page 13). To make the waves in the top of the comb, pinch the sides of the comb in and needle the top more firmly at intervals (see page 13), making four or five waves, with a larger one in the center.

3 Follow Basic Body 3 (see page 16) to make a light gray wing on either side of the body, making them 1¼in (3cm) long and ¾in (2cm) wide at the widest point. For the tail, fold a weft of light gray into a strip and fold that in half. Needle the loose ends to the chicken's rear end, leaving the loop standing up. Add three or four loops of different sizes, as shown. Needle some small pieces of white wool between the loops to add a bit of volume and fluffy texture (see page 20).

4 For the beak, make a tiny cone of orange/yellow wool on the foam block (see page 10) and attach it just below the start of the comb. Make spots of black wool for the eyes (see page 18), taking care that they are level when seen from the front.

5 Add a thin strip of dark gray wool all the way around the edge of each wing, then add a few stripes along the length. Add a stripe of dark gray between each loop of the tail, and use just a few strands of dark gray wool to make a number of light dashes down the chicken's breast.

SAFETY NOTE

Since the chicken has a polystyrene ball in its core, it is not safe for children under 3 years old to play with.

Lay a little EGG for me!

Diving Duck

This colorful little duck is a mallard, the most common dabbling duck in the northern hemisphere. The male duck, known as a drake, has beautiful iridescent feathers in blues and greens that are great fun to create with felting.

You will need

Merino wool in
white 0.35oz (10g)
light green 0.18oz (5g)
maroon 0.18oz (5g)
dark green 0.07oz (2g)
light blue 0.07oz (2g)
dark blue 0.07oz (2g)
dark pink 0.07oz (2g)
light brown 0.18oz (5g)
black 0.07oz (2g)
banana-yellow 0.18oz (5g)
orange 0.07oz (2g)

Carded wool in
dark gray 0.18oz (5g)
light gray 0.18oz (5g)

Felting needle with handle

Foam block

Sharp embroidery scissors

Techniques Checklist

Basic Body 2 page 15
Applying Color page 18
Padding Shapes page 13
Shaping Pieces page 13
Basic Body 3 page 16
Making Basic Shapes: Ears, Tails, and Wings page 10
Making an Eye page 20

1 Follow the first stages of Basic Body 2 to join the body and head (see page 15), making an egg-shaped body measuring 3in (8cm) long by 2in (5cm) wide at the fattest point, using white wool. Make a head measuring 2 x 1in (5 x 2.5cm) from light green wool in the shape shown, and join it to the body with a weft of white. Then wrap a weft of green over the head only, without changing the shape (see page 18).

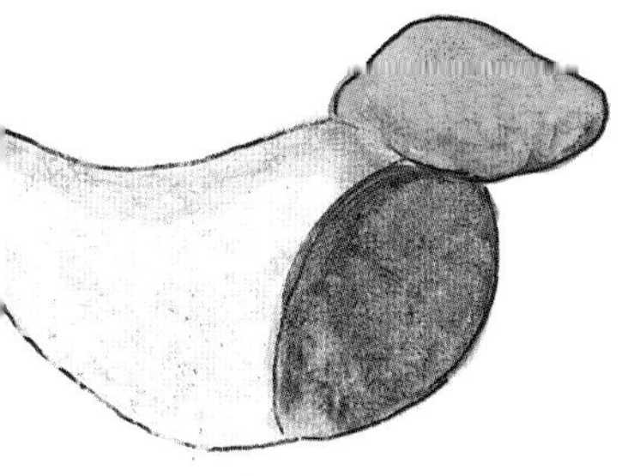

2 Pad the chest out (see page 13) with folded wefts of dark gray carded wool. Add a layer of light gray carded wool to the rest of the body. Shape the back and tail by pinching and needling them into shape (see page 13), making a gentle curve in the back and a rounded point for the tail.

3 Add a folded weft of maroon wool to the chest area in the shape shown, working over the dark gray and under the body. Cover the crown of the head with small wisps of dark green and light and dark blue wool (see page 18), lightly blending them so that they are mottled.

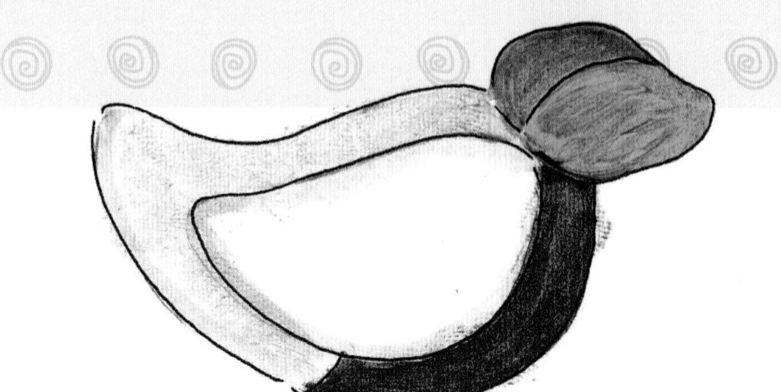

4 Using light gray carded wool, follow Basic Body 3 (see page 16) to make the wings. Make them 2½in (6cm) long and 1¼in (3cm) across at the widest point and position them as shown, taking care that they are symmetrical on the sides of the body.

5 Start to build even more color. Add a few wisps of dark pink to the chest (see page 18). Lightly shade the wings with short wisps of white merino wool. Add a bit of blue wool above and below the wings, toward the tail end. Add a wisp of light brown wool on the duck's back, starting at the neck. As you needle the color on, shape the back further toward the point of the tail (see page 13).

6 At the top of each wing, from about two-thirds of the way along and going up to the point of the tail, add a triangle of black wool. Add a few dots of white to the black area (see page 19). Shade in the bottom of the tail and tummy with white wool, squeezing and needling the tail further to curve it up into the classic shape of a rubber duck. Extend the white wool to curve up around the front of each wing.

7 Curl up a wisp of banana-yellow wool and needle it into the rough shape of a bill, in the same way that you would make a tail or ear (see page 8), leaving some loose fibers for attaching it at the base. Needle it to the head around the base. Flatten the bill with your fingers and needle it to make the shape more defined (see page 13). Add small pieces of black wool for the nostrils and tip of bill detail. Then add a short wisp of white wool to outline the base of the bill. Needle underneath the bill to make the inward curve of the neck.

8 Needle on a pea-sized piece of black wool for each eye and a white dot for the highlight (see page 20), taking care that the eyes are level when seen from the front. Add a wisp of light green above the eyes for the eyelids. Needle on a thin line of white wool around the neck (see page 19).

9 Fold a weft of orange wool and needle the folded end into a flat diamond shape (see page 10), 1in (2.5cm) wide. Needle the loose end into a strip for the leg, leaving loose fibers at the end. Repeat to make two feet.

10 Hold one foot flat against the tummy, pointing toward the tail, and attach the loose fibers to the tummy, as in the leg on the left of the drawing. Then fold the other leg over so that the foot points toward the head and needle the leg to hold it in that position. Check that the duck sits level when you have attached both feet.

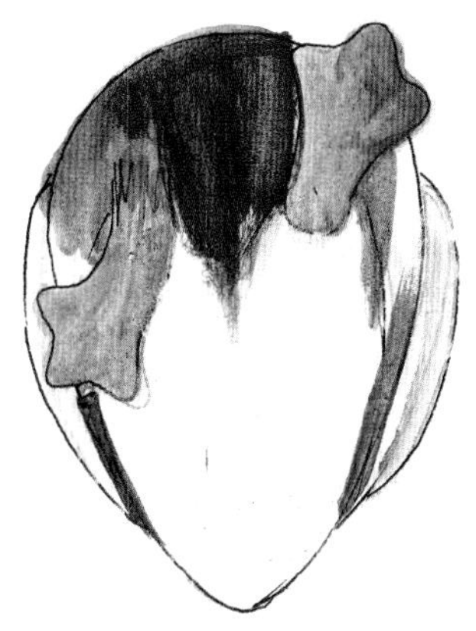

Quack, QUACK, quack!

Wide-Eyed Owl

There are many beautiful species of owl, with different markings and colorings. The instructions show you how to make a tawny colored owl but you can use white wool to make the snowy owl, if you prefer.

1 Follow Basic Body 3 (see page 16), making the body and head from white merino wool and the wings from gray carded wool. The body measures 2¾in (7cm) long by 2½in (6cm) wide at the fattest point, and the wings are 2¾ x 1⅜in (7 x 3.5cm). The head is 1in (2.5cm) high. Do not make the tail yet. Attach the wings and head to the body, making them the shape shown.

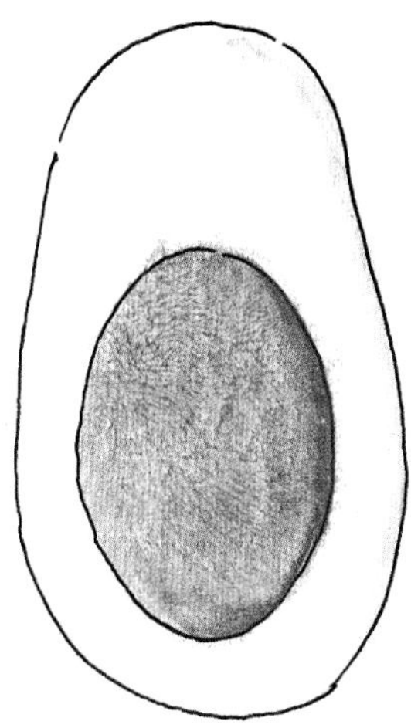

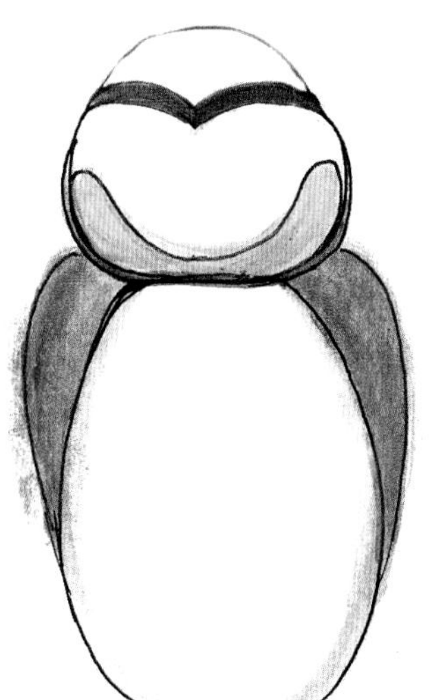

2 Pull off a piece of light brown wool and roll it between your forefinger and thumb to make a strip. Then, starting from the center of the forehead ¾in (2cm) down from the top of the head, attach the strip to make the heart-shaped face outline. Hold the strip with one hand and guide it into place with the needle (see page 19). Now add some light beige alpaca wool to the inside edge of the heart shape.

Twit TWOOOOO!

You will need

Merino wool in
white 0.35oz (10g)
light brown 0.18oz (5g)
peach 0.01oz (0.5g)
light yellow 0.01oz (0.5g)
dark purple 0.01oz (0.5g)
light green 0.01oz (0.5g)
black 0.07oz (2g)

Carded wool in dark gray 0.18oz (5g)

Alpaca wool in
light beige 0.03oz (1g)
white 0.07oz (2g)

Felting needle with handle

Foam block

Sharp embroidery scissors

Techniques Checklist

Basic Body 3 page 16
Applying Color page 18
Making an Eye page 20
Padding Shapes page 13
Adding Fluffy Texture page 20
Making Basic Shapes: Legs and Tails page 9
Joining Basic Shapes page 11

3 Add some peach and a few strands of light yellow merino wool to the cheeks. Shade the back of the head, the owl's back, and just under the chin to the edges of the wings with light brown wool, leaving the chest white.

4 For the eyes, roll a small piece of dark purple wool in between your forefinger and thumb to make a strip. Attach the strand in a small circle, $\frac{5}{8}$in (1.5cm) wide. Fill the circle with light green merino wool, then needle on a small piece of purple wool in the center of the circle for the owl's pupil. Add a white wool highlight (see page 20).

5 To create the beak, pull off a pea-sized piece of black wool and attach it $\frac{3}{8}$in (1cm) up from the center bottom of the outlined face shape, overlapping it onto the chest by about $\frac{1}{4}$in (0.5cm). Needle it around the edges into a pointed sausage shape (see page 13), then add more wool to build it up into a 3-D beak.

6 Add white alpaca wool to the chest, brow, and above the beak, keeping the wool fluffy (see page 20). Add a bit of light beige alpaca to the brow and then more white alpaca on top. Use a wisp of the light brown merino wool to create tiny tear shapes on the chest, guiding the strands into the right shape with the needle (see page 18). Lightly needle on a few strands of peach to soften the markings.

7 On the back of the head, the top of the back, and the wings, use tiny wisps of white merino wool to make little dashes of color, applying them in the same way as for the chest spots, and angling them to follow the curves of the body. Add a strand of brown wool to the top of the head, as shown.

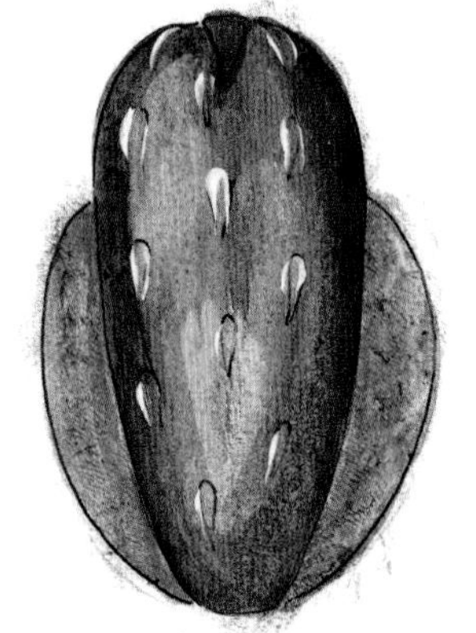

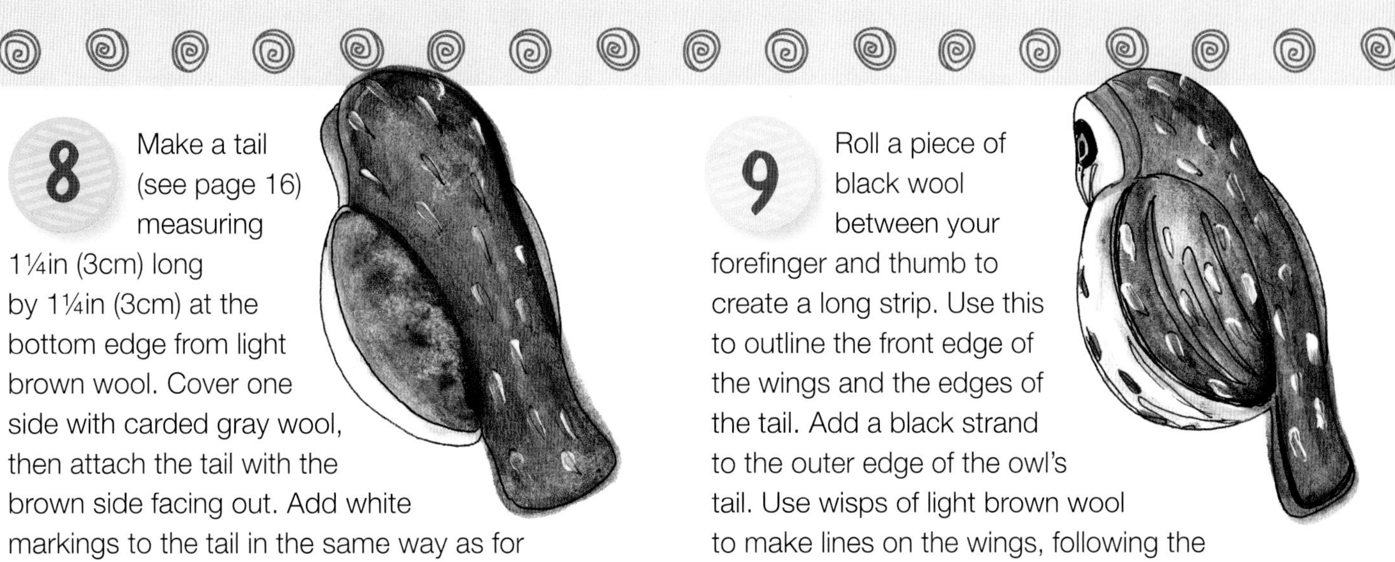

8 Make a tail (see page 16) measuring 1¼in (3cm) long by 1¼in (3cm) at the bottom edge from light brown wool. Cover one side with carded gray wool, then attach the tail with the brown side facing out. Add white markings to the tail in the same way as for the head and back.

9 Roll a piece of black wool between your forefinger and thumb to create a long strip. Use this to outline the front edge of the wings and the edges of the tail. Add a black strand to the outer edge of the owl's tail. Use wisps of light brown wool to make lines on the wings, following the outlined shape.

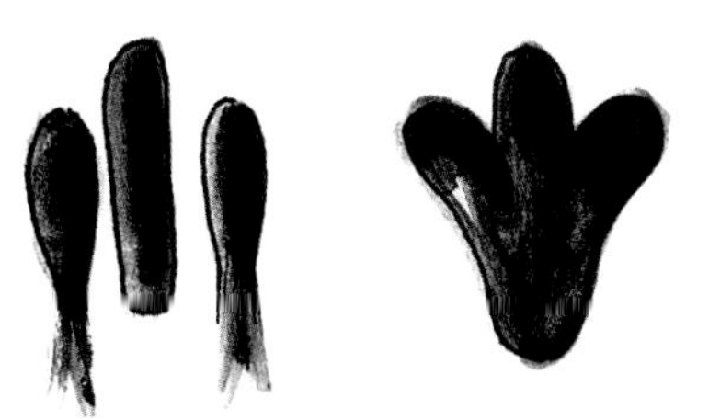

10 For the feet, make a small black wool sausage, 1¼in (3cm) long (see page 9). Make two shorter sausages for the toes, leaving loose fibers on one end. Attach the loose fibers to the longer sausage to make a three-toed foot (see page 11), as shown.

11 Finally, needle the feet to the bottom of the owl so that the toes just peak out from under the tummy.

Colorful Parrot

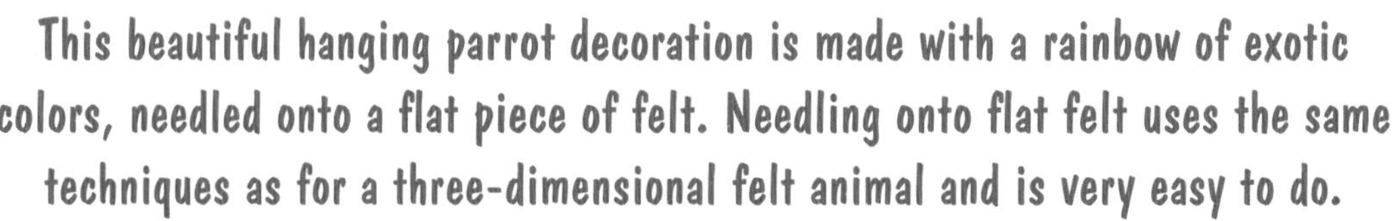

This beautiful hanging parrot decoration is made with a rainbow of exotic colors, needled onto a flat piece of felt. Needling onto flat felt uses the same techniques as for a three-dimensional felt animal and is very easy to do. Parrots live mainly in tropical and subtropical climates and are brightly colored and very smart—some of them can copy sounds and voices.

You will need

Template on page 127

8 x 8½-in (20 x 22-cm) sheet of black felt

Soft graphite pencil, marker pen, or fabric chalk

Merino wool in golden-yellow 0.07oz (2g), light green 0.20oz (6g), teal 0.18oz (5g), white 0.10oz (3g), maroon 0.03oz (1g), orange 0.07oz (2g,) light blue 0.03oz (1g), light turquoise 0.03oz (1g), dark pink 0.07oz (2g), red 0.10oz (3g), dark blue 0.07oz (2g), black 0.03oz (1g)

Carded wool in light gray 0.07oz (2g)

Felting needle with handle

Foam block

Sharp embroidery scissors

Iridescent seed and bugle beads and beading needle

Sewing needle and black thread (optional)

Thin black ribbon

Fabric glue

Techniques Checklist

Flat Felting page 17
Applying Color page 18
Padding Shapes page 13
Making an Eye page 20

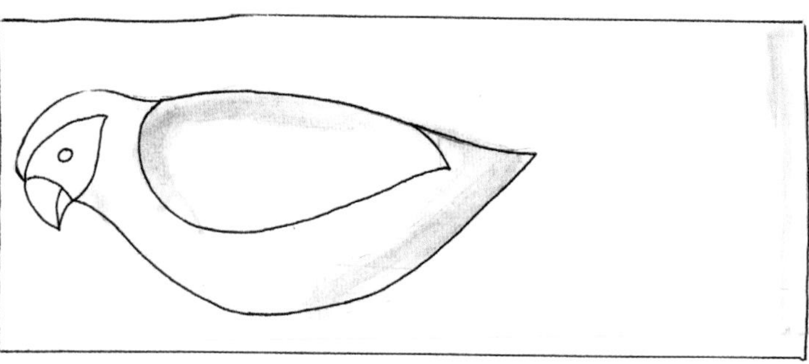

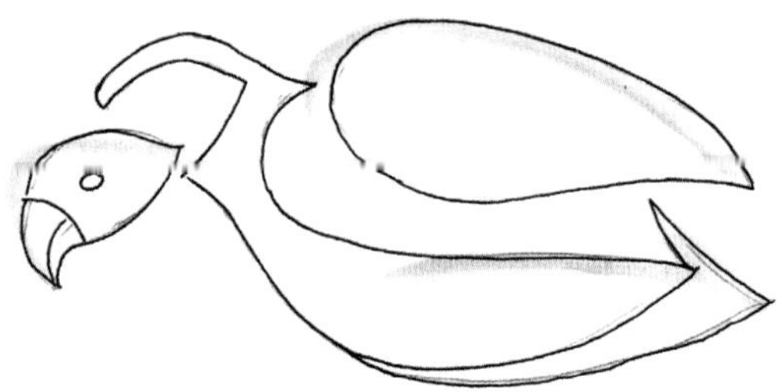

1 Fold the felt in half to find the center line and cut into two rectangles. Copy and cut out the template. Lay one rectangle flat and place the template in the center so there is a narrow border all the way around. Draw around it using a pen that shows on the black. Don't cut it out. Next, cut out the wing, head, and beak shapes from the paper template. Position them inside the felt outline and draw around them onto the felt.

TIP

While felting, remember to regularly pull the felt off the foam block to prevent it becoming attached.

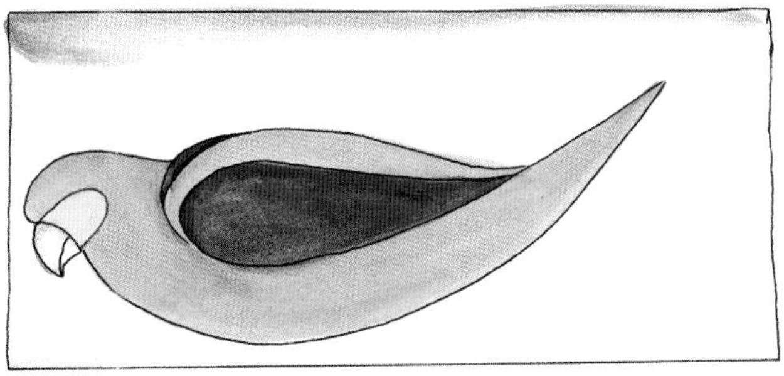

2 With a few wisps of yellow, fill in the face area (see page 18). Cover the whole body apart the wing and beak with light green wool. Build up the chest with a few folded wisps (see page 13). Use the same wool to extend the tail by 2in (5cm) in the shape shown. Fill in the wing with teal wool, with a folded wisp of light green wool on the outside edge. Shade in the beak with a few bits of gray carded wool.

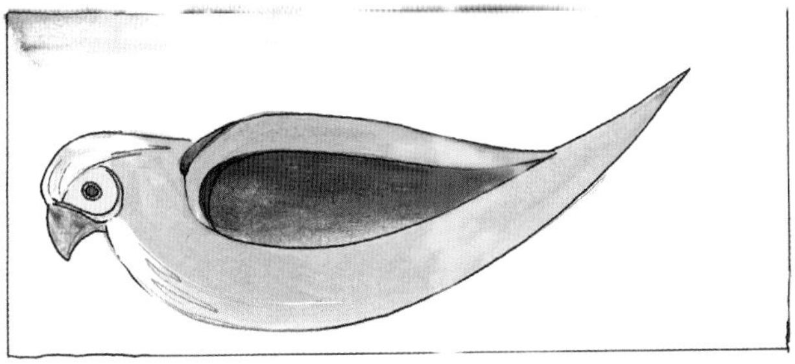

3 Add a few wisps of white wool to the top and back of the head, a few strands around the lower edge of the face by the beak, and a few wispy bits under the beak down to the chest (see page 18). Make a spot of maroon wool for the eye, then outline that first in orange, then in white. Add a white highlight in the eye (see page 20).

All the COLORS of the rainbow

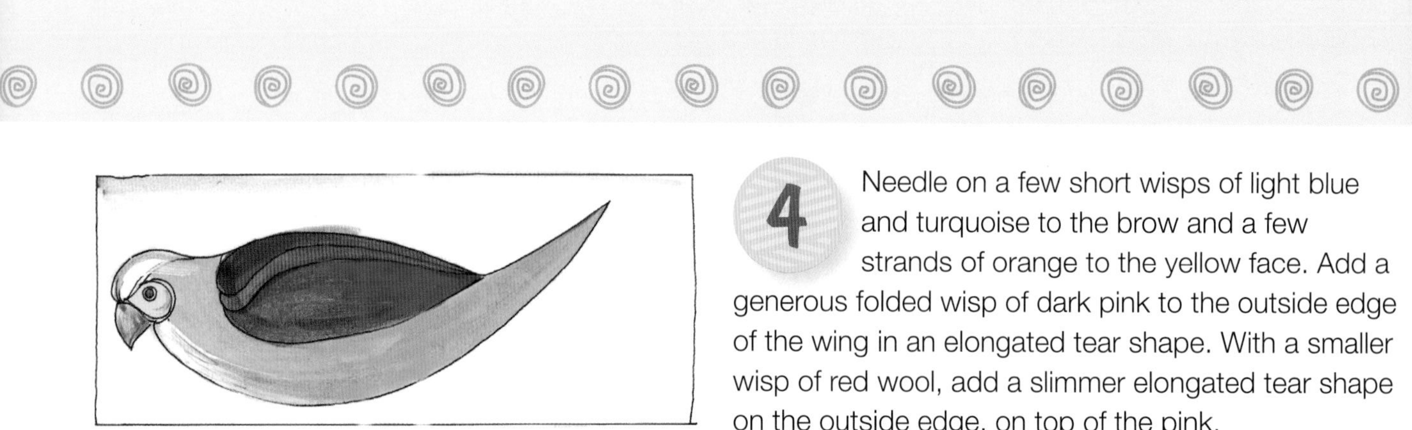

4 Needle on a few short wisps of light blue and turquoise to the brow and a few strands of orange to the yellow face. Add a generous folded wisp of dark pink to the outside edge of the wing in an elongated tear shape. With a smaller wisp of red wool, add a slimmer elongated tear shape on the outside edge, on top of the pink.

5 With the light green wool, add two more long feather shapes to the tail end, one 3½in (9cm) long and the other 4in (10cm) long, so that they stick out from the body. Outline each feather with a strip of red, fading it on the inside edge, and add a few wisps of orange and pink to each feather.

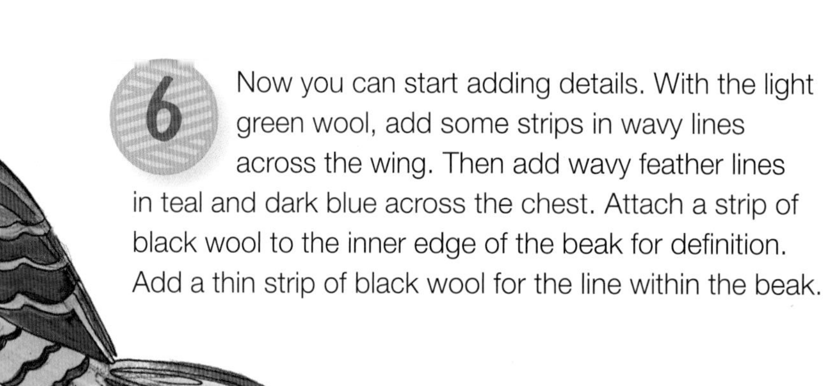

6 Now you can start adding details. With the light green wool, add some strips in wavy lines across the wing. Then add wavy feather lines in teal and dark blue across the chest. Attach a strip of black wool to the inner edge of the beak for definition. Add a thin strip of black wool for the line within the beak.

7 With your sharp scissors, cut out the parrot shape from the black felt, leaving a narrow margin around the edge for the outline. Using a needle and black thread, sew beads to the wing in whatever arrangement you like.

8 To sew on a bead, thread a beading needle (or a sewing needle thin enough to pass through the bead) and knot the end of your thread. Bring the needle through the felt from the back to the front where you'd like your bead to sit. Thread the bead onto the needle and down the thread so that it rests against the felt. Take the needle back through the felt where it first came out, and bring it out a bead length along, pulling the thread so that the bead is held in place. Repeat this stitch to secure the bead. To attach another bead, don't cut the thread but simply bring the needle out again at the next place and sew on a bead in the same way.

TIP
You can choose your beads in the same colors as the wools, or use lots of different colors if you wish.

9 To make the backing piece, draw around the parrot on the remaining piece of black felt and cut out the shape. Cut a length of thin black ribbon measuring 8in (20cm) long for the hanging loop. Fold the ribbon in half and glue or sew the ends onto the backing piece where the wing meets the back of the neck. Apply glue to the back of the colored parrot and place it on the backing, sandwiching the ends of the loop in between. Let it dry. If you like sewing, you could blanket stitch the front and back of the parrot together instead of gluing.

chapter 3

Country Critters

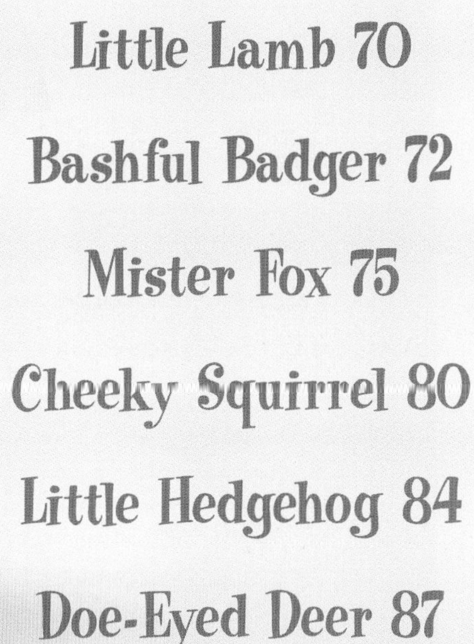

Little Lamb

This fluffy little character makes a great Easter decoration, or an adorable gift for someone. Change up the colors to make a black sheep if you like. For a soft and natural effect you can use real sheep fleece, or keep it simple with merino wool.

You will need

Raw washed sheep fleece in white 0.35oz (10g) (optional)

Carded wool in
dark gray 0.18oz (5g)
light gray 0.03oz (1g)

Merino wool in
white 0.18oz (5g)
peach 0.07oz (2g)
black 0.07oz (2g)

Carding combs or two dog brushes

Felting needle with handle

Foam block

Sharp embroidery scissors

Techniques Checklist

Basic Body 2 page 15
Joining Basic Shapes page 11
Blending Joined Shapes page 12
Shaping Pieces page 13
Making Basic Shapes: Bodies and Heads page 8
Making Basic Shapes: Ears, Tails, and Wings page 10
Applying Color page 18
Making an Eye page 20

1 If using the white raw washed fleece, prepare it by brushing the wool in opposite directions between carding combs or dog brushes, to get rid of any debris and to separate the fibers and fluff up the wool.

2 Using the prepared fleece or white merino wool, follow Basic Body 2 (see page 15), to make an egg-shaped body measuring 2¾in (7cm) long by 2in (5cm) wide at the fattest point. Make a head measuring 1⅜ x ¾in (3.5 x 2cm) from dark gray carded wool, making it the shape shown. Join the body and head with a weft of the carded washed fleece.

3 Using four equal-sized pieces of carded dark gray wool, make four legs, each measuring 2in (5cm) long and ⅝in (1.5cm) thick. Fold the loose fibers at the top of each leg over at a right angle and attach them to the underneath of the fluffy body (see page 11), not to the sides. Make sure all the legs are the same length so the lamb stands level without toppling. Cover the join with a generous weft of carded fleece (see page 12).

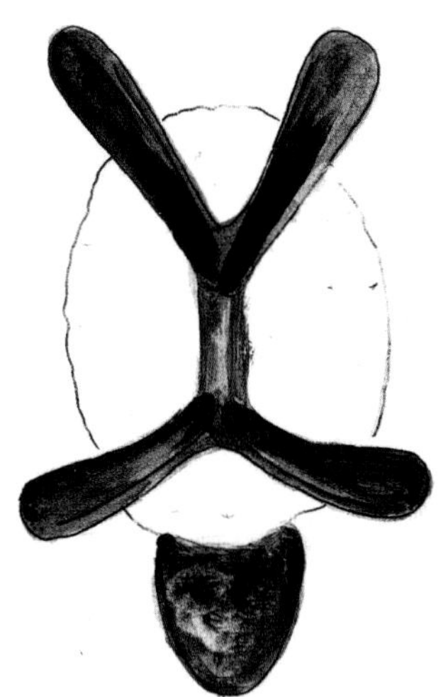

Full of the joys of SPRING!

4 Arrange the legs as shown and needle the sheep's tummy to hold them in position (see page 13). Make a ⅜-in (1-cm) ball of carded washed fleece (see page 8) and attach it to the rear end for a tail. Lightly needle a few wisps of white merino wool over the body to give it a baby-soft texture.

5 For the ears, use dark gray wool to make two flat discs measuring ⅝in (1.5cm) across (see page 10). Attach these to the sides of the head where the head joins the white body. Shade the inside of each with a wisp of peach wool (see page 18).

6 To shape the face, pinch the sides together and needle in the shape of the brow, muzzle, and mouth area (see page 13). Needle in the eye sockets, then use a pea-sized bit of white merino wool to add an almond-shaped eye in each socket. Add black irises and white highlights (see page 20).

7 Blend a little light gray wool over the front of the mouth and muzzle area (see page 18), then add an upside-down triangle of peach wool for the nose. Outline the sloping sides of the nose with black, then use a sliver of black for the mouth; start by needling on the middle of the strand just under the nose, and then guide the ends into place with the needle.

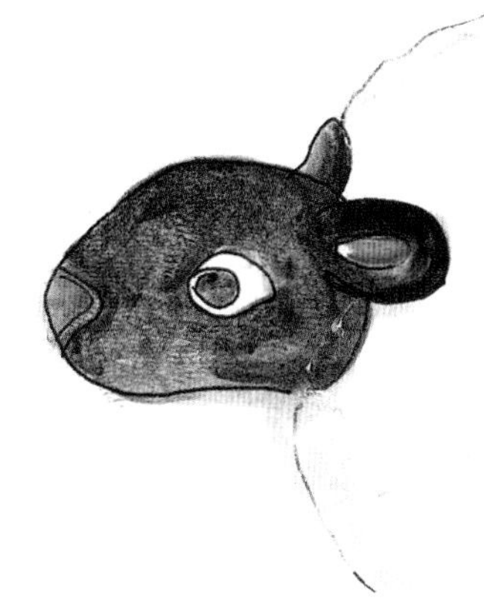

Bashful Badger

This handsome creature is easy to shape, giving you more time to spend on his stripy head and wise expression. Many badgers live underground in a set and are nocturnal, only coming out at night.

You will need

Carded top wool in
dark gray 0.70oz (20g)
light gray 0.35oz (10g)

Merino wool in
black 0.35oz (10g)
white 0.35oz (10g)

Alpaca wool in
white 0.18oz (5g) (optional)

Gray and black mix silk fibers
0.35oz (10g) (optional)

Felting needle with handle

Foam block

Sharp embroidery scissors

Techniques Checklist

Basic Body 2 page 15
Padding Shapes page 13
Applying Color page 18
Shaping Pieces page 13
Making Basic Shapes: Ears, Tails, and Wings page 10
Joining Basic Shapes page 11
Blending Joined Shapes page 12
Adding Ears page 21
Making an Eye page 20
Adding Fluffy Texture page 20

1 Make a Basic Body 2 (see page 15), making an egg-shaped body measuring 3in (8cm) long by 2¼in (5.5cm) wide at the fattest point from carded dark gray wool. Make the head measuring 1¾ x ¾in (4.5 x 2cm) from black wool, making it the shape shown.

2 Join the body and head with a weft of dark gray wool. Lay a wide weft of light gray wool over the neck and back, and needle this in to make the body's contours smooth and plump (see page 13). Add more black wool to the chest (see page 18). Make the legs 2in (5cm) long and ⅝in (1.5cm) thick and attach them beneath the body (see page 12).

3 Add a few wisps of black wool to the insides of the legs. Bend over the very tips of the legs, making sure that the badger is balanced. Pinch and needle the ends into position to create the paws (see page 13). Create a flat, oval tail (see page 10) measuring ¾ x ⅝in (2 x 1cm) from dark gray wool and attach it to the badger's rear end (see page 11). Add a wisp of light gray to join and blend the tail to the body (see page 12).

4 Add a teardrop-shaped area of white merino wool to each side of the badger's head (see page 18), with the pointed end of the teardrop toward the nose; keep the wool loose and fluffy on the cheeks. Then add a folded wisp of white wool in a stripe down the snout. Add a bit more black wool to darken the two stripes running on either side of the snout up to the top of the head.

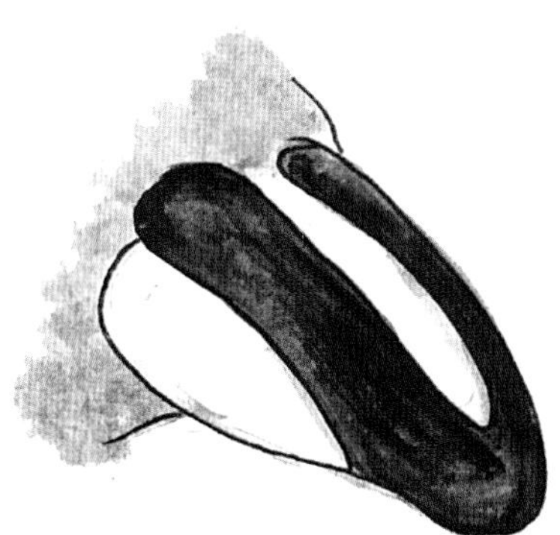

WISE old badger

5 Make the ears from pea-sized balls of white merino with a wisp of black wool on the inside. Attach an ear at the top of each black stripe on the head (see page 21), pinching the shape as you fuse the fibers. Add wisps of black to blend the insides of the ears into the stripes.

6 For the eyes, attach small dots of white wool about ⅜in (1cm) down the black stripes from the ears. Add black pupils to the eyes, leaving the white underneath as highlights and add dark gray eyelids (see page 20). Make sure that the highlight is in the same place in each eye.

7 Pull off a small piece of dark gray wool for the nose and needle it into an upside-down triangle on the end of the snout.

8 If you'd like to give the badger wispy fur, add a few wisps of white alpaca to the cheeks and the top of the head, keeping it light and fluffy, and add short wisps of the silk fibers to the whole of the back area, needling them on very lightly (see page 20).

Mister Fox

In this more advanced project, you will practice modeling the legs and tail from chenille stems, which makes them adjustable so that you can pose your fox in lots of different ways, from sitting to running. His handsome face is built up from detailed colors, shaping his eyes and muzzle to give him a cunning gaze.

You will need

Five chenille stems (pipe cleaners)

Carded top wool in
gray 0.35oz (10g)

Merino wool in
dark orange 0.70oz (20g)
white 0.18oz (5g)
bright orange 0.18oz (5g)
black 0.18oz (5g)
dark brown 0.07oz (2g)
light yellow 0.07oz (2g)
light brown 0.03oz (1g)

Alpaca wool in
white 0.07oz (2g)

Felting needle with handle

Foam block

Sharp embroidery scissors

Techniques Checklist

Making Basic Shapes: Bodies and Heads page 8
Applying Color page 18
Needling Wool around a Skewer page 18
Basic Body 1 page 14
Padding Shapes page 13
Shaping Pieces page 13
Adding Fluffy Texture page 20
Making Basic Shapes: Ears, Tails, and Wings page 10
Adding Ears page 21
Making an Eye page 20

FANTASTIC Mr Fox!

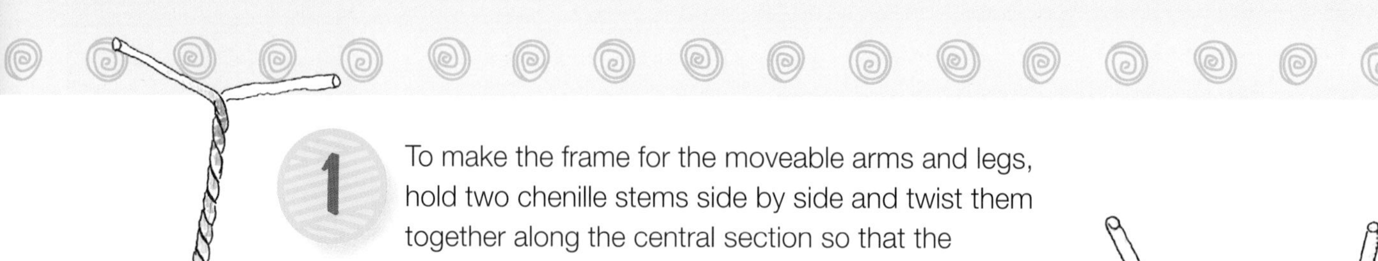

1 To make the frame for the moveable arms and legs, hold two chenille stems side by side and twist them together along the central section so that the twisted section is about 2in (5cm) long.

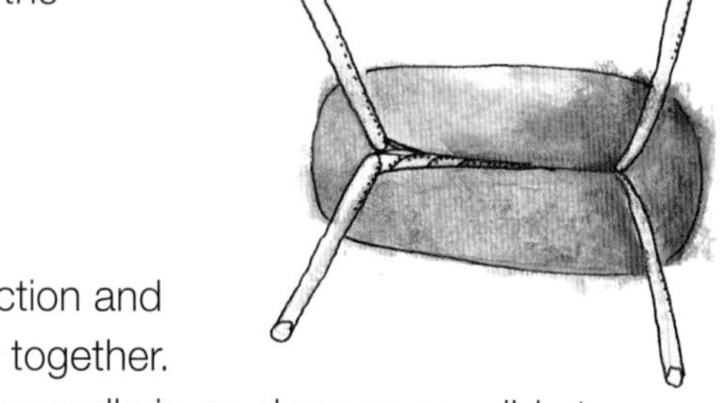

2 From carded gray wool, make an egg shape measuring 3½in (9cm) long for the body (see page 8). With your fingers, open up the underside of the body just a little and push the frame in, so that the twisted section is inside the body and the loose ends of the stems stick out. Pinch the body closed over the twisted section and needle it firmly together. Try to push the needle in as close as possible to both sides of the stems to embed them firmly in the wool. Cover the whole body with dark orange wool (see page 18), making sure it is smooth over the underside.

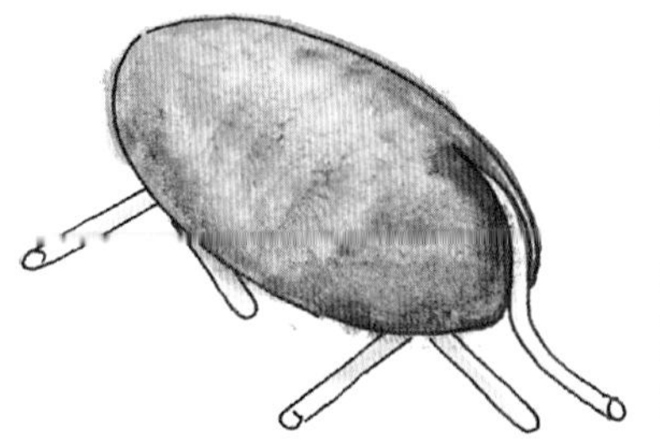

3 For the fox's tail, place a chenille stem along the spine, starting about ⅜in (1cm) from the narrow end of the body. Bend the chenille stem into a lightly bent shape as shown, and trim it as needed with scissors. When you are happy with the length and position, lay a weft of dark orange wool over the fox's back and needle it on firmly to hold the tail frame in place.

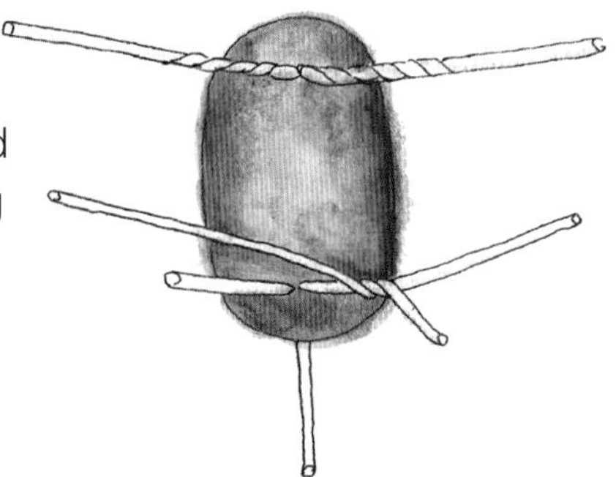

4 Use the remaining two chenille stems to lengthen the legs and make them sturdier. Twist one chenille stem around and along each pair of legs, as shown. Then needle a large weft of dark orange wool over the belly to cover where the leg frames emerge.

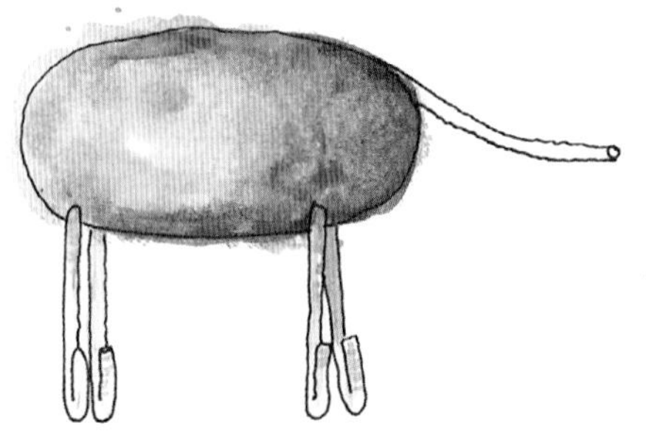

5 Bend the legs down so that they are in the correct positions below the body, adding more wool to the belly if needed to cover the frame. Bend over about ⅜in (1cm) of the bottom of each stem for the paws. Make sure that all the paws are level so that the fox can stand up without toppling.

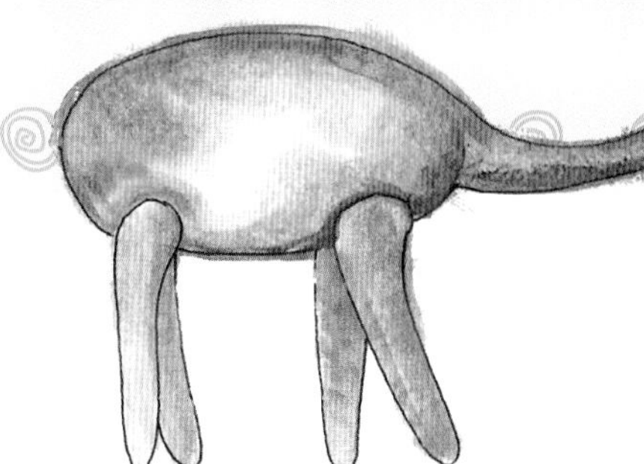

6 Take a generous weft of the gray carded wool and cover each leg up to where it joins the body. Needle-felt the wool around the chenille stem in the same way as you would around a skewer (see page 18), pinching in the wool as you go and being careful not to prick yourself. Concentrate on the paw area to make sure that the stems are completely hidden, and make sure that the wool is all fully felted so the legs look slender, not chunky. Do the same with dark orange wool on the tail, blending the base of the tail into the body.

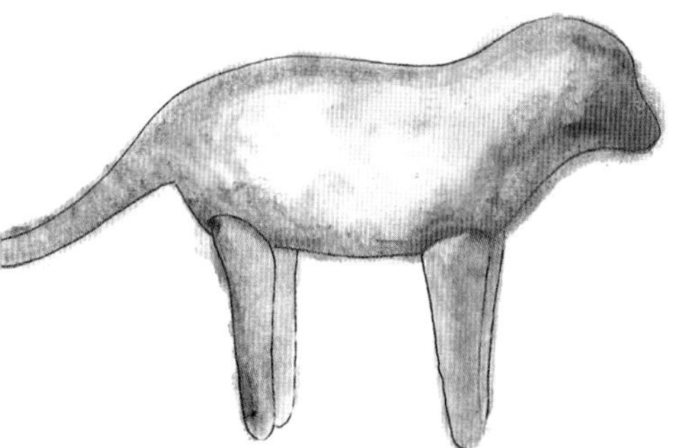

7 Follow Basic Body 1 (see page 14) to make a neck about ¾in (2cm) long and a head about 1½in (4cm) long from dark orange wool. The neck needs to be smoothly rounded and blended into the body, as shown, so add wefts of wool to achieve the right shape (see page 13). The muzzle is quite long and needs to be kept rounded and angled down. Pinch the top of the muzzle into shape while you needle to create the defined slope of the bridge of the nose (see page 13).

8 Take a generous weft of dark orange wool to create the haunch for each leg. Shape the weft into a large teardrop with your fingers, then lay it in position with the rounded end over the top of the leg, and needle it in around the edges to secure it (see page 13). Then lightly needle over and around the whole piece until it has a smooth, rounded surface. Work on both the front and back legs to create the shapes shown.

9 Add white wool, starting from just under the chin, carrying on down in between the front legs, and filling in the tummy to just under where the tail joins on (see page 18). Keep the chest rounded and work the needle more in the tummy area so that it curves inward (see page 13). Add a small piece of white wool under the muzzle and another to the tip of the tail.

TIP

If the tail is a bit skinny, pad it out with more orange wool before adding the white tip.

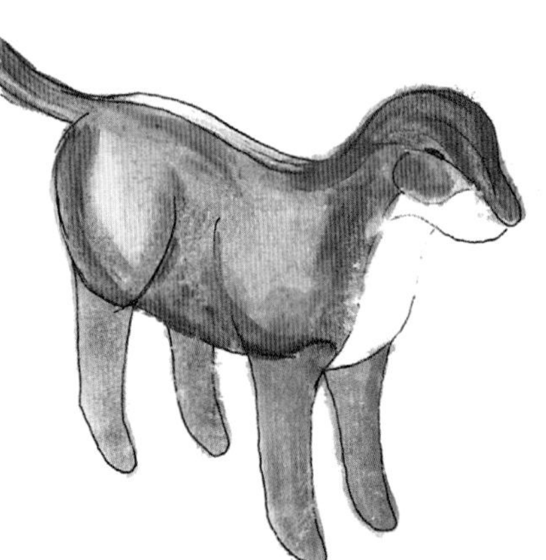

10 Add a little bright orange wool to shade the bridge of the nose, the top of the head, down the back of the neck, the back, and onto the tail. With embroidery scissors, trim back any orange that covers the white tail tip. Needle the bright orange on lightly, so that it stays soft and fluffy (see page 20).

11 Add black wool to each leg, making sure that the paws are completely black and the color fades up to the top of the leg (see page 18). Needle on a piece of dark brown wool around the top of each leg, blending it in. Then add a small piece of bright orange to the outside of each haunch, fading it out to leave the brown and black shading showing through.

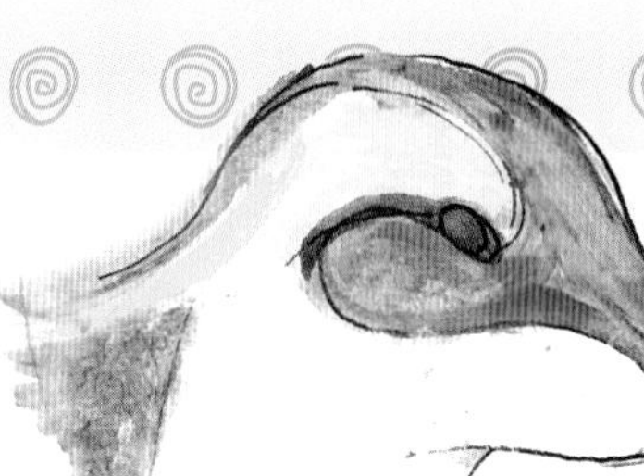

12 Add more white wool to the fox's cheeks to build up the head shape. Needle some light yellow wool onto the nose, the brow, and the outer edge of the white chest area. Then add some bright orange to the eye socket and nose, and in an upside-down arrow shape on the forehead. Fill in the eye sockets with dark brown wool.

13 Use the carded wool to make two flat, teardrop shapes, each about ¾in (2cm) long (see page 10). Needle the base of each ear to the head around the back and inside edges (see page 21). Lay the fox on the foam block and needle the ears into shape; try to keep them curved and pinch them while needling to shape the pointed tips. Add some dark orange and bright orange wool to the backs to blend them into the back of the head. Color in the insides with white wool, then add some strands of dark brown wool to the outer edges (see page 18).

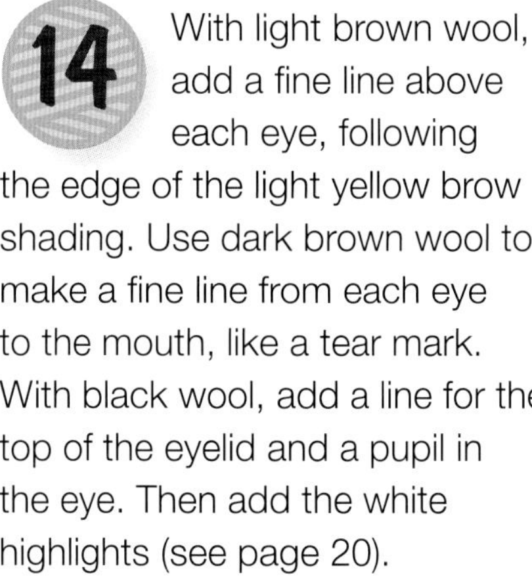

14 With light brown wool, add a fine line above each eye, following the edge of the light yellow brow shading. Use dark brown wool to make a fine line from each eye to the mouth, like a tear mark. With black wool, add a line for the top of the eyelid and a pupil in the eye. Then add the white highlights (see page 20).

15 Use black wool to add an upside-down triangle for the nose; keep adding black wool until the nose protrudes and looks good on the fox's profile. Add a sliver of black wool for the mouth; start by needling on the middle of the strand just under the nose, and then guide the ends into place with the needle. Add small tufts of alpaca white wool to the cheeks, chest, and brow, leaving them fluffy (see page 20).

Cheeky Squirrel

There are more than 200 species of squirrels across the world, giving you plenty to choose from to recreate in felt! Our squirrel has gray fur but you could easily change this to red, if you prefer.

You will need

Carded wool in
mottled gray 0.70oz (20g)

Merino wool in
white 0.07oz (2g)
light brown 0.07oz (2g)
peach 0.07oz (2g)
charcoal 0.03oz (1g)
golden-yellow 0.07oz (2g)

Alpaca wool in
white 0.18oz (5g)
fawn 0.07oz (2g)
beige 0.18oz (5g)
gray 0.07oz (2g)

Felting needle with handle

Foam block

Sharp embroidery scissors

Techniques Checklist

Basic Body 2 page 15
Shaping Pieces page 13
Padding Shapes page 13
Applying Color page 18
Joining Basic Shapes page 11
Blending Joined Shapes page 12
Making Basic Shapes: Ears, Tails, and Wings page 10
Adding Ears page 21
Making an Eye page 20
Making Basic Shapes: Bodies and Heads page 8

1 The squirrel is based on Basic Body 2 (see page 15), but it is sitting rather than standing. Make an egg-shaped body measuring 3in (8cm) long by 2¼in (5.5cm) wide at the fattest point from gray carded wool. Make the head measuring 2 x 1⅜in (5 x 3.5cm) from the same wool, making it from a cone of loose wool to get the shape shown. Join the body and head with a thin weft of gray wool.

2 Make the legs 2¾in (7cm) long and ⅝in (1.5cm) thick and attach them with 2⅝in (6.5cm) of the front legs sticking out beyond the body and only 1¾in (4.5cm) of the back legs sticking out. Needle the bottom of the body flat, so that the squirrel can sit upright (see page 13).

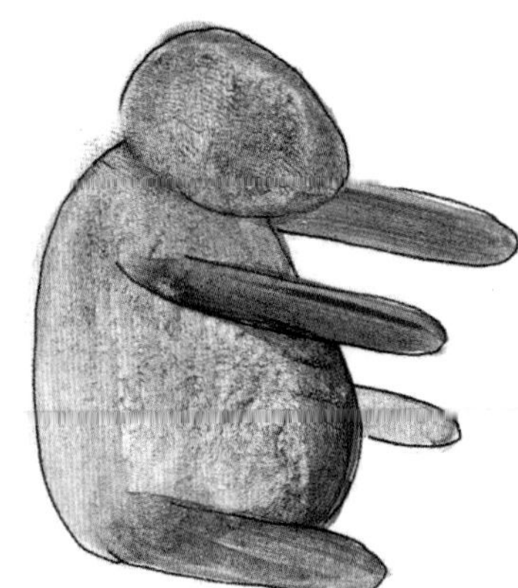

3 Bend the arms upward at a right angle to make the elbows, and twist them so that the paws meet together in the middle. Squeeze and needle the elbows so that they hold this position (see page 13). Add a folded weft of gray wool to each upper arm to build them up (see page 13). Add three folded wefts to each haunch, needling to make them full and smoothly rounded. Flatten the ends of the arms and legs to make the paws.

BUSHY tailed and bright eyed

4 Curl the whole body inward in your hand, squeezing it into a ball shape so that the nose touches the paws. As you do this, needle around the neck and all around the back to curl the squirrel; it will straighten up a bit when you let go of it. Apply a few wefts of white merino wool, then a few wefts of white alpaca wool to the tummy. Then add a little bit of brown merino to the back and to the crease at the top of the haunches for definition (see page 18).

5 On the foam block make a roughly oval pillow measuring 2¼in (5.5cm) wide, 5¼in (13.5cm) long, and 1in (2.5cm) deep from carded gray wool for the tail. Attach this to the back of the squirrel just above the top of the haunches (see page 11). Then add a few fluffed-up wefts to the bottom of the tail to blend it into the body (see page 12). Shape the tail into a swishy curve with your fingers and the needle. Add a layer of gray alpaca fleece to the front and back of the tail.

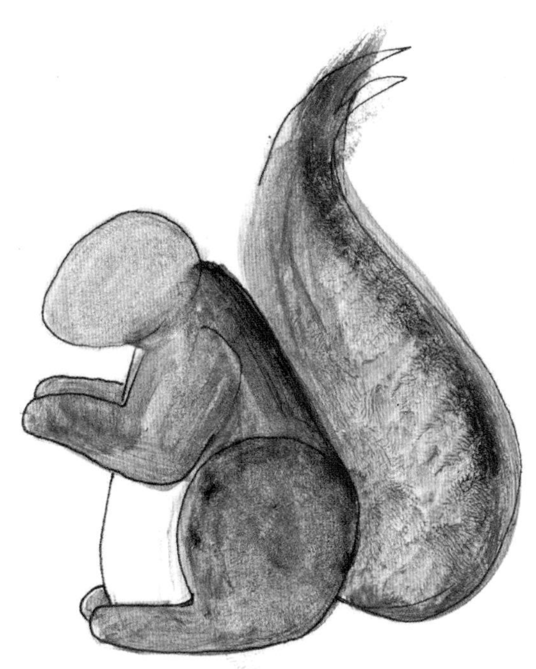

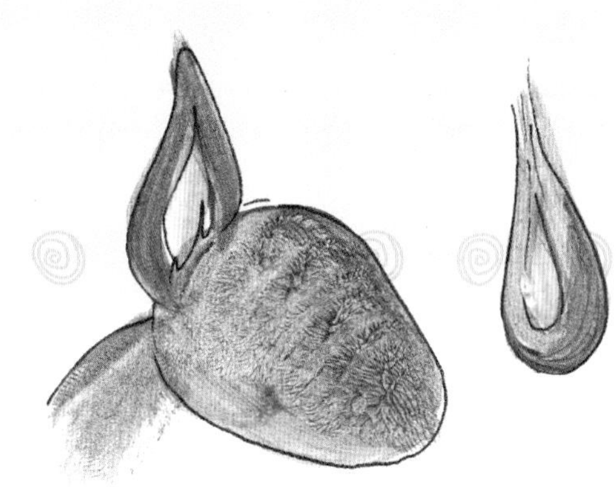

6 Make two flat, triangular shapes measuring 1¼ x 1¾in (3 x 4.5cm) from gray carded wool (see page 10) for the ears. Shade the insides with brown wool and a layer of peach, then add a strip of charcoal wool around the edge (see page 18). On the foam block, squeeze the edges of each ear inward and needle down the center to fold the ear inward, working the tip of the ear to a point. Attach the ears to the sides of the squirrel's head. Add a wisp of gray wool to the back to blend and smooth the join (see page 21).

7 Squeeze and needle the head to a point for the nose and make the eye sockets (see page 13), then pad out the cheeks and the mouth area with white merino (see page 13). Add a pea-sized bit of charcoal wool in an oval in the eye sockets, and a little peach wool around the eyes, fading it out onto the cheeks. Work the needle under the chin to shape it, then pinch and needle the end of the muzzle to make it narrower and to indent the mouth.

8 Outline the eye with fawn alpaca, then add a white merino highlight (see page 20). Add a thin line of brown wool under each eye. Needle in a wisp of fawn alpaca on the bridge of the nose for shading. Add a curved line of brown for the nose and a thin line of dark gray for the mouth; start by needling on the middle of the strand just under the nose and then guide the ends into place with the needle. Add three lines of charcoal to the paws to define the toes.

9 For the acorn, using the golden-yellow wool, make a small egg shape measuring 1¼ x ¾in (3 x 2cm) (see page 8). Then add a piece of light brown wool wrapped around the top to create the cap. Needle it in until it is smooth, then add a few strands of black for detail. Add a light brown sausage for the stalk. Place the acorn between the squirrel's paws.

TIP

If your squirrel doesn't have a tight grip, you may need to needle the arms inward a little more to help hold the nut!

Little Hedgehog

With soft tufts of wool for spines, this is one little baby hedgehog that you can pick up and cuddle! Baby hedgehogs are known as hoglets and their favorite food is bugs, such as worms, caterpillars, and slugs!

You will need

Carded wool in
dark mottled gray 0.18oz (5g)
light mottled gray 0.03oz (1g)

Merino wool in
white 0.10oz (3g)
dark brown 0.07oz (2g)
light brown 0.07oz (2g)
peach 0.18oz (5g)
black 0.18oz (5g)

Felting needle with handle

Foam block

Sharp embroidery scissors

Techniques Checklist

Making Basic Shapes: Bodies and Heads page 8
Applying Color page 18
Making Basic Shapes: Necks and Beaks page 10
Joining Basic Shapes page 11
Shaping Pieces page 13
Extending Shapes page 13
Making Basic Shapes: Ears, Tails, and Wings page 10
Adding Fluffy Texture page 20
Adding Ears page 21
Making an Eye page 20

1 Start by making an egg shape measuring 2⅞ x 1¾in (7.5 x 4.5cm), in dark gray wool for the body (see page 8). The narrow end will be the top and the fat end the base of body. Cover one side of the body with white wool (see page 18); this will be the tummy.

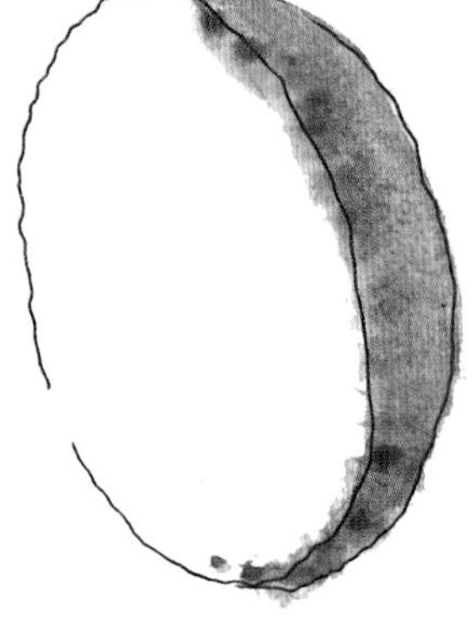

2 Curl a wisp of white wool into a cone shape for the head (see page 10). Needle the base of the cone onto one end of the white part of the body (see page 11). Needle the nose lightly, pinching in the tip with your fingers while you needle (see page 13). Then wrap a wisp of white around the nose and needle it to build up the shape (see page 13).

3 Needle in dips for the eye sockets on either side and just above the nose. Wrap a piece of dark brown wool around the tip of the nose and needle it on. Then wrap a light brown wisp of wool around the nose just below the dark brown to finish the snout, as shown.

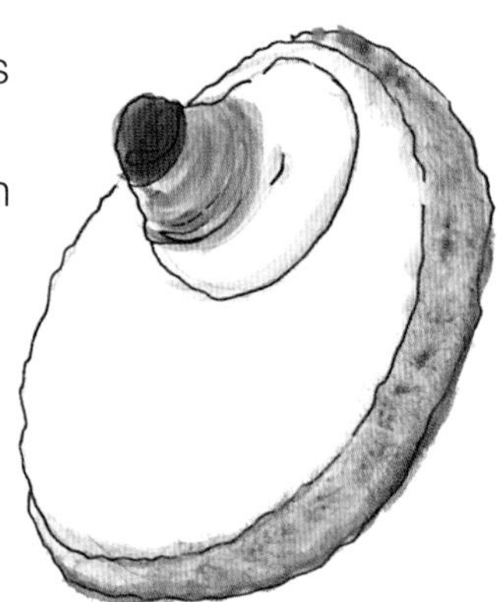

4 From peach wool create four slim, flat ovals for the legs (see page 10), each measuring 1⅜ x ⅜in (3.5 x 1cm), with loose fibers at one end. Attach the fibers to the body so that the legs are at slanting angles pointing upward and outward, as shown (see page 11).

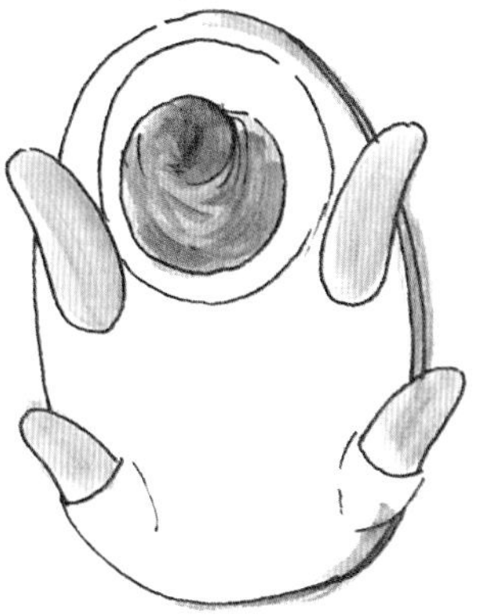

Roll up, ROLL UP!

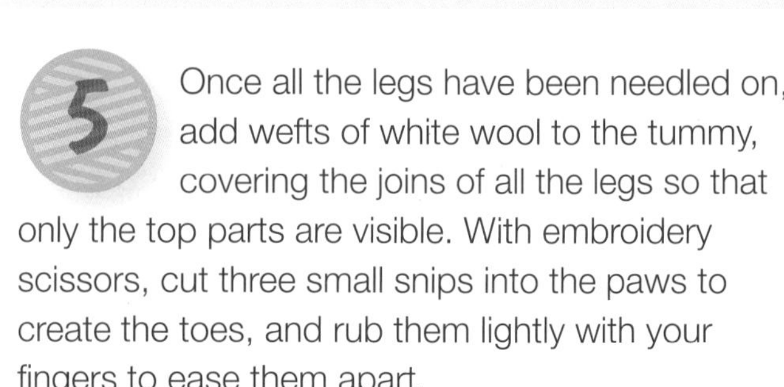

5 Once all the legs have been needled on, add wefts of white wool to the tummy, covering the joins of all the legs so that only the top parts are visible. With embroidery scissors, cut three small snips into the paws to create the toes, and rub them lightly with your fingers to ease them apart.

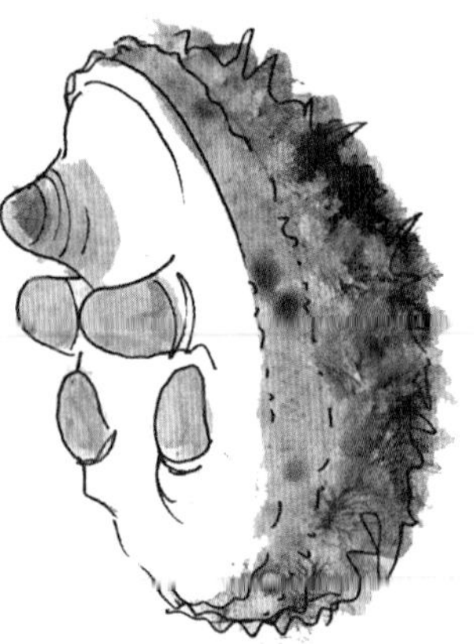

6 Add a weft of dark gray wool to the back to build up the shape, needling the wool lightly to keep it soft and fluffy (see page 20). Curl the body inward while needling to give the hedgehog a rounded shape. Add a few wisps of light gray and light brown around the edges of the body to blend together the white and dark gray (see page 18).

7 Pull off two pea-sized pieces of dark brown wool and make two flat ovals for the ears (see page 10). Needle the two shapes into place as shown (see page 21), then add a wisp of white wool to the inside of each ear. Needle a wisp of light brown wool into each eye socket and then add a smaller wisp of black on top. Then add a few strands of white wool for the highlight in each eye (see page 20).

8 Add a few short wisps of white wool to the top of the head, cheeks, and tummy, lightly needling them in place. Finally, trim any unwanted fuzz with embroidery scissors. You can position your hedgehog on its back with its legs waving in the air, or balanced upright on its bottom.

Doe-Eyed Deer

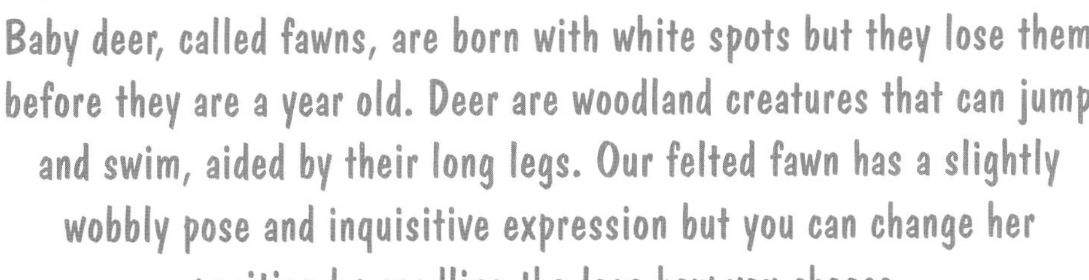

Baby deer, called fawns, are born with white spots but they lose them before they are a year old. Deer are woodland creatures that can jump and swim, aided by their long legs. Our felted fawn has a slightly wobbly pose and inquisitive expression but you can change her position by needling the legs how you choose.

You will need

Merino wool in
peach 0.90oz (25g)
dark brown 0.07oz (2g)
light brown 0.10oz (3g)
orange/yellow 0.01oz (0.5g)
white 0.01oz (0.5g)
pink 0.03oz (1g)
black 0.07oz (2g)

Felting needle with handle

Foam block

Sharp embroidery scissors

Techniques Checklist

Basic Body 1 page 14
Shaping Pieces page 13
Padding Shapes page 13
Making Basic Shapes: Legs and Tails page 9
Adding Ears page 21
Applying Color page 18
Extending Shapes page 13
Making an Eye page 20

1 Make a Basic Body 1 (see page 14), making an egg-shaped body measuring 3½in (9cm) long by 1¼in (3cm) wide at the fattest point from peach wool. Make the neck 2in (5cm) long and the head 1½ x ¾in (4 x 2cm) from peach wool, making them the shapes shown. Make the legs 2⅝in (6.5cm) long and ⅜in (1cm) thick and attach them with 1¾in (4.5cm) hanging below the body—make sure that the deer's rear end protrudes beyond the back legs.

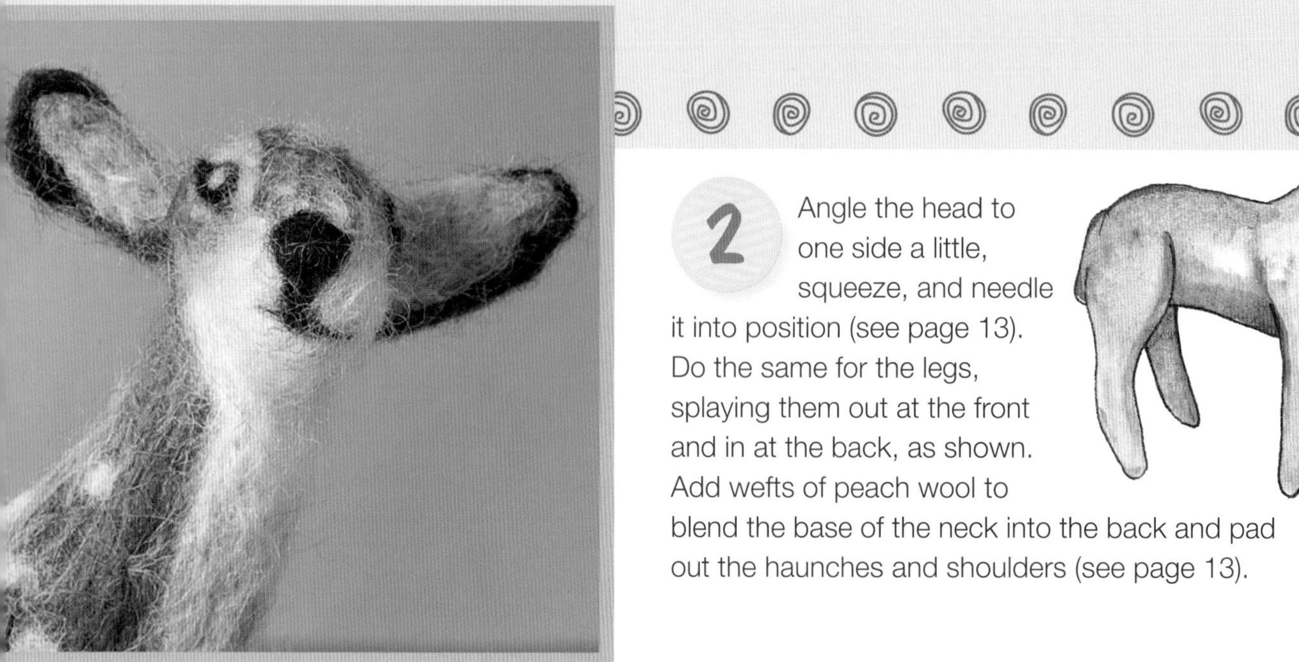

2 Angle the head to one side a little, squeeze, and needle it into position (see page 13). Do the same for the legs, splaying them out at the front and in at the back, as shown. Add wefts of peach wool to blend the base of the neck into the back and pad out the haunches and shoulders (see page 13).

3 Make a small peach wool sausage (see page 9) and attach it to the deer's rear end for the tail. Using dark brown wool, make two flat teardrop shapes for the ears, measuring 1in (2.5cm) long. Needle them onto the head around the curved end, keeping the tips pointed (see page 21).

4 Add light brown shading to the deer's back, then up the back of the neck to the top of the head and down the muzzle (see page 18). Add brown on the outside of the legs to about halfway down, fading it out to the ankle. Shade the sides of the face and the chest with the orange/yellow wool and put a few strands on the back.

5 Add some white wool to the chest, keeping it light and thin so that the colors underneath show through. Cover the belly and the inside of the legs with white, taking the color around under the tail, and blending the edges. Add a few strands on the outside of the legs, allowing some peach and brown to show through. Add some white wool to the chin and cheeks, making the chin stick out a little (see page 13). Add some pink to the inner ears, some strands of white to the outer ears, and some black to the tips. Needle a few strands of white onto the top of the head.

6 Needle in the eye sockets and pinch and needle the muzzle to shape it. Shade in around the eye down to the chin with light brown. Use pea-sized balls of white wool to make slightly slanting, almond-shaped eyes. Then add a smaller black almond-shaped iris and a thin black outline. Add a highlight in each eye (see page 20).

7 Add an upside-down triangle in black for the nose (see page 18), then needle on a little more black wool to make the nose stick out slightly. Add a small sliver of black wool for the mouth: needle on the strand in the center just under the nose and then guide the rest of it into place with the needle.

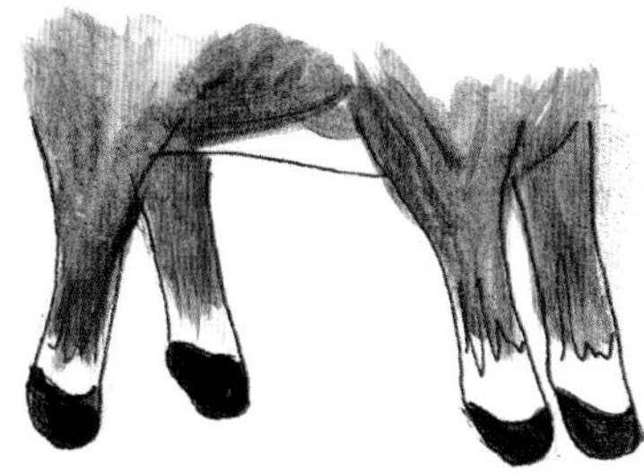

8 Using the embroidery scissors, cut the tips of the legs at a 45-degree angle to make the hoof shape. Pinch and needle the hoof so that the tip is slightly pointed (see page 13). Then add black wool for the hooves, adding more wool at the front and less at the back.

9 For the markings, add some dark brown and peach strands to the back of the deer's neck. Then add white dots all over the deer's back and some peach spots around the rear end, making them slightly different sizes and not too big (see page 19).

chapter 4

Playful Pets

Cool Cat Brooch

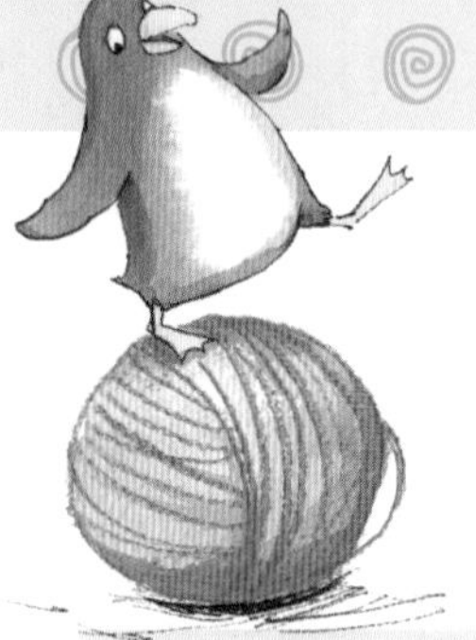

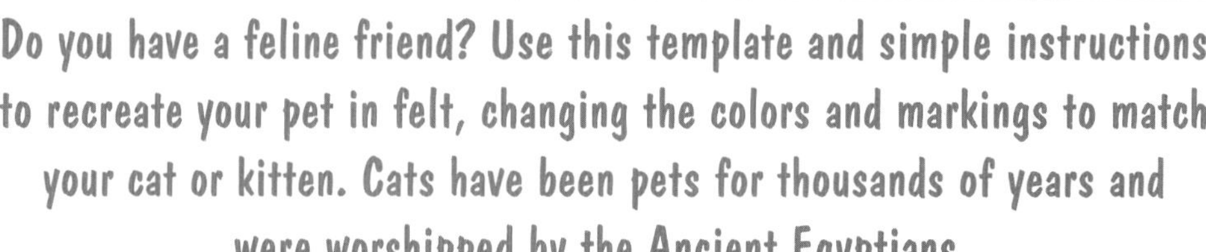

Do you have a feline friend? Use this template and simple instructions to recreate your pet in felt, changing the colors and markings to match your cat or kitten. Cats have been pets for thousands of years and were worshipped by the Ancient Egyptians.

You will need

Template on page 126

8 x 4-in (20 x 10-cm) sheet of black felt

Soft graphite pencil, marker pen, or fabric chalk

Merino wool in
golden-yellow 0.14oz (4g)
light brown 0.10oz (3g)
peach 0.03oz (1g)
dark pink 0.03oz (1g)
light turquoise 0.03oz (1g)
black 0.18oz (5g)
light yellow 0.10oz (3g)
white 0.07oz (2g)

Felting needle with handle

Foam block

Sharp embroidery scissors

Fabric glue

Brooch finding 1¼in (3cm) long

Sewing needle and black cotton thread (optional)

Techniques Checklist

Flat Felting page 17
Applying Color page 18
Padding Shapes page 13
Making an Eye page 20
Adding Fluffy Texture page 20

1 Fold the felt in half to find the center line and cut it into two 40-in (10-cm) squares. Copy the template on page 126 and cut out the shape. Place the template on one square of black felt, near the edge, allowing a small border all around. Draw around the template with a pen that shows up on the felt. Don't cut it out. Next, cut out the eyes and nose shapes from the paper template and draw around these in position inside the head outline.

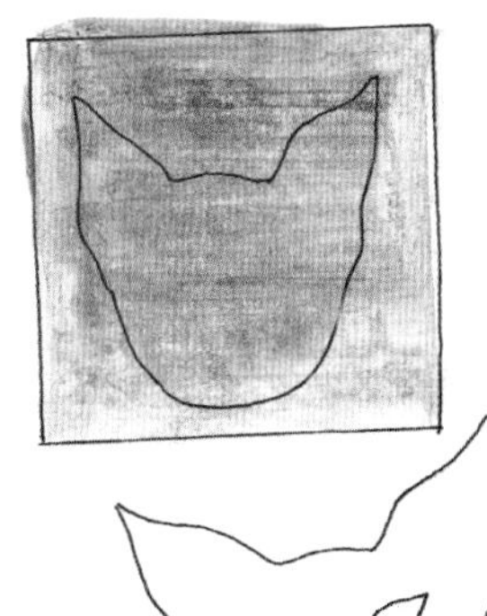

2 Use wisps of golden-yellow wool to fill in the face, except for the eyes, nose, and inside the ears (see page 18). Add a few short folded wisps of light brown running down from the top of the head to the nose. Then add some light brown wool to the outside edge of the head and along the inside bottom line of the ears. Shade the insides of the ears with a few wisps of peach wool.

3 Add a pea-sized piece of dark pink wool for the nose. Color in the eyes with the light turquoise wool, then give them a heavy black outline, bringing it out at the inner and outer corners. Add a second outline of light yellow wool outside the black line. Needle on three small balls of light yellow wool for the cat's top lip and chin (see page 13). Needle the edges of the balls to blend them into the base.

4 Add thin lines of black wool for the mouth and the whiskers. In light brown, needle on a few soft lines running down from the top of the head to just above the brow, then add a few strands of light yellow, and finally a few strands of black. Add strands of light brown to the cheeks and temples, then add thin black lines for the cheekbones and across the base of the inner ears.

5 Make elongated pupils from black wool and add white highlights (see page 20). Outline the whole head in black. Finally, add a few short, fluffy wisps of light yellow and white to the inside of the ear, leaving them lightly felted (see page 20).

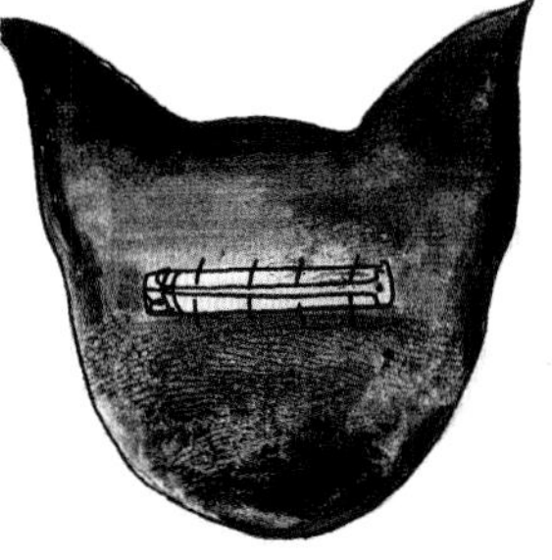

6 Cut out the finished cat's head, leaving a narrow margin around the edge to give it a black outline. Lay it on the second square of black felt and draw around it, then cut out the shape for backing. Glue or sew the brooch finding to the middle of the backing. Apply glue to the back of the colored cat and place it on the backing, with the brooch finding on the back. Let the glue dry, then needle on a few strands of black wool over the edge to make it fluffy.

TIP

If you like sewing, you could blanket stitch the front and back of the brooch together instead of gluing.

COOL for CATS

Happy Hamster

This sweet little rodent is quick and easy to make with a simple body shape. Hamsters make great pets as they are so entertaining, running in a wheel or scampering through tunnels. They are mostly active at night—at least your felted pet won't keep you awake!

You will need

Merino wool in
white 0.35oz (10g)
burnt orange 0.07oz (2g)
peach 0.18oz (5g)
bright orange 0.10oz (3g)
brown 0.03oz (1g)
pink 0.18oz (5g)
black 0.03oz (1g)

Felting needle with handle

Foam block

Sharp embroidery scissors

Techniques Checklist

Basic Body 2 page 15
Applying Color page 18
Making Basic Shapes: Ears, Tails, and Wings page 10
Adding Ears page 21
Making an Eye page 20
Making Basic Shapes: Legs and Tails page 9
Joining Basic Shapes page 11
Blending Joined Shapes page 12

1 Make a Basic Body 2 (see page 15) from white wool, making an egg-shaped body measuring 3¼in (8.5cm) long by 1¾in (4.5cm) wide at the fattest point. Make the head 1⅜ x ¾in (3.5 x 2cm), positioning it on the body as shown and blending the two together with a weft of white wool. Add another weft if needed to make the head and body one smooth shape.

2 Wrap a weft of burnt orange wool over the back and another over the tummy, leaving the nose area white (see page 18). Needle the wool until it is smooth over the body, then add a few wisps of peach wool on top of the burnt orange, followed by a few wisps of bright orange. Use a wisp of white wool to create the heart-shaped face centered on the nose. Extend the white in a stripe down the chest to the tummy.

KEEP ON running!

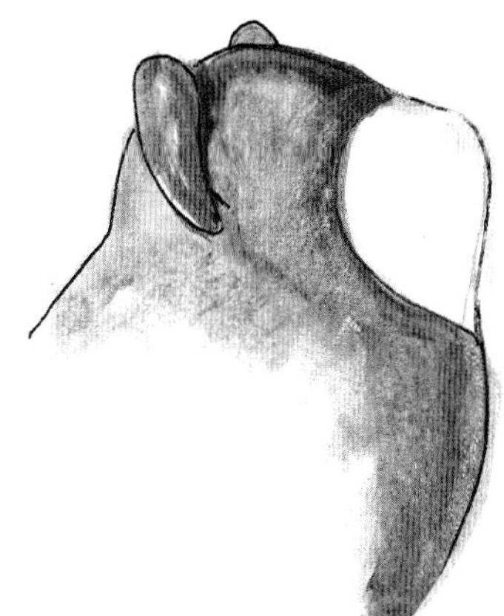

3 For the ears, pull off two pea-sized pieces of peach wool and make two small, flat ovals (see page 10). Attach the ears to the top of the head, leaving a ⅝-in (1.5-cm) gap between (see page 21), checking that they are level.

4 Needle in around the base of the back of the ears, then add a wisp of bright orange to blend and shade in the backs. Add a strand of brown wool around the edge of the ears, then add a few strands of white inside them (see page 18).

5 Add wisps of bright orange and brown wool running down the head to the peak at the top of the white face. Make the nose from a wisp of pink wool, then add a slither of pink to make the mouth, needling it on in the center then guiding it into place with the needle (see page 18). Use wisps of black wool to make the eyes, positioning them just above the cheeks with a ⅝-in (1.5-cm) gap in between them. Then add a few strands of white wool for the highlights (see page 20).

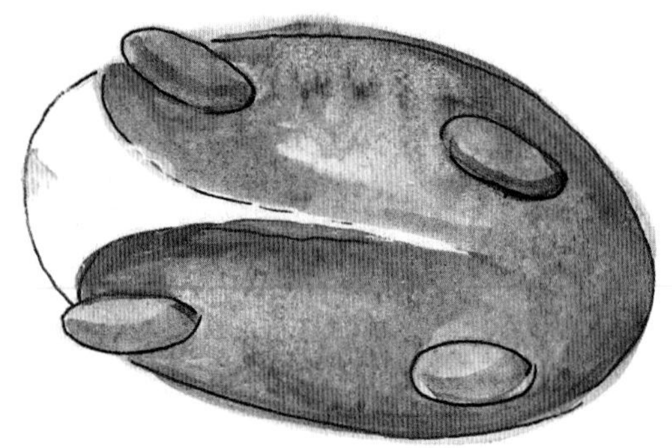

6 For the feet, make four pink wool sausages measuring 1 x ¼in (2.5 x 0.7cm), and one thin sausage ⅝in (1.5cm) long for the tail (see page 9). Needle the feet into position on the bottom of the body, as shown (see page 11).

7 Lay a wisp of bright orange wool over the bottom of the front feet and needle it in so that just the tips of the feet are visible. Attach the tail to the hamster's rear end and add a wisp of bright orange wool to blend it into the body (see page 12).

TIP

Change the wool colors to make a white or brown hamster, if you prefer.

Dashing Dog Brooch

This handsome dog is a German Short-haired Pointer. His elegant head makes a great shape for flat felting and you can turn him into a brooch or make a picture from him in a box frame. Pair him up with the cat brooch on page 92 for extra pet style.

You will need

Template on page 126

8 x 4-in (20 x 10-cm) sheet of black felt

Soft graphite pencil, marker pen, or fabric chalk

Merino wool in
light brown 0.18oz (5g)
black 0.18oz (5g)
orange 0.03oz (1g)
maroon 0.03oz (1g)
white 0.07oz (2g)

Carded wool in
dark mottled gray 0.18oz (5g)
light mottled gray 0.07oz (2g)

Felting needle with handle

Foam block

Sharp embroidery scissors

Fabric glue

Brooch finding 1¼in (3cm) long

Sewing needle and black cotton thread (optional)

Techniques Checklist

Flat Felting page 17
Applying Color page 18
Making an Eye page 20
Making Basic Shapes: Ears, Tails, and Wings page 10
Joining Basic Shapes page 11

1 Fold the felt in half to find the center line and cut it into two 4-in (10-cm) squares. Copy the template on page 126, cut out the shape, and place it on one square of felt, leaving a small border. Draw around the template with a pen that shows up on the felt. Don't cut it out.

2 Fill in the entire area with light brown wool (see page 18). With strips of black wool, outline the head shape and jaw line. Add a few wisps of dark gray carded wool to the muzzle, and a few strands of orange and maroon merino wool on the top of the head.

TIP
While felting, remember to pull the felt off the foam block once in a while to prevent it from becoming attached.

3 Add a bit of light gray carded wool to the muzzle, extending it up toward the eye, then add a black wool nose (see page 18). To create the dog's eye, add a small oval of white wool, as shown in the illustration. Add a black line to the top of the eye.

4 Add an orange wool iris to the left corner of the white eye, then add a black pupil (see page 20). Needle on a thin black line under the eye, and a bit of white underneath that, then add the thin black line that defines the cheekbone. Add more light gray to the muzzle, and some to the neck.

5 Cut the ear shape out of the paper template. Using brown wool, make a flat shape on the foam block, about the same size as the ear template, needling it until it is quite solid (see page 10). Add a few strands of light gray. Place the paper template over the felt shape and cut out the ear.

6 Attach the ear to the head, needling it on all over (see page 11). Outline the ear in black, then add a little white wool to the front edge of the ear and to the muzzle. Add a few strands of orange and maroon to the top edge of the ear.

7 Add some dots of white wool to the ear and some brown and white dots on the neck area (see page 19). Needle on a few strands of black below the nose and add a few to the eye and cheek lines if they have become blurred.

8 Cut out the finished dog's head, leaving a narrow margin around the edge to give it a black outline. Lay it on the second square of black felt and draw around it, then cut out the shape for a backing. Glue or sew the brooch finding to the middle of the backing piece. Apply glue to the back of the colored dog and place it on the backing. Let the glue dry, then needle on a few strands of black wool over the edge to make it look fluffier.

TIP

If you like sewing, you could blanket stitch the front and back of the brooch together instead of gluing.

A HANDSOME hound!

Faithful Spaniel

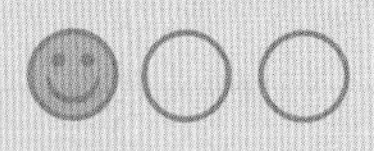

Spaniels are fun and lively, making great playmates that will always be at your side. There are lots of different markings and breeds to choose from, so have fun making your own unique faithful friend in felt.

You will need

Merino wool in
white 0.70oz (20g)
light brown 0.10oz (3g)
chestnut-brown 0.10oz (3g)
burnt orange 0.01oz (0.5g)

Alpaca wool in
white 0.10oz (3g)
fawn 0.07oz (2g)

Silk fibers in blond 0.03oz (1g)

Felting needle with handle

Foam block

Sharp embroidery scissors

Techniques Checklist

Basic Body 2 page 15
Shaping Pieces page 13
Padding Shapes page 13
Extending Shapes page 13
Making Basic Shapes: Legs and Tails page 9
Joining Basic Shapes page 11
Applying Color page 18
Making Basic Shapes: Ears, Tails, and Wings page 10
Adding Ears page 21
Making an Eye page 20
Adding Fluffy Texture page 20

1 From white merino wool make a Basic Body 2 (see page 15), making an egg-shaped body measuring 3in (8cm) long by 2in (5cm) wide at the fattest point. Make the head measuring 2 x 1¼in (5 x 3cm) from the same wool, making it the shape shown. Make the legs 2¾in (7cm) long and ⅜in (1cm) thick and attach them to the body, with 1¾in (4.5cm) hanging below the body, making sure that they are level.

2 Make the paws by bending over the tips of the legs by ⅜in (1cm) and needling them into position (see page 13). Bend the knees backward as shown and needle them into position, then check that the dog stands level without toppling. Build up the haunches and shoulders by adding curled wefts of white wool to them (see page 13). Pad out the legs by wrapping wefts around them, making sure that the legs stay in position.

3 Add wool to make the rear end rounded, and add another weft around the neck join to smooth it further. Add folded wefts of white wool to pad out the chest. Squeeze and needle in the curves of the back and the tummy. Needle in the bridge of the nose, muzzle, and eye sockets, then wrap a wisp of white wool around the muzzle to build it up and lengthen it (see page 13). Finally, wrap wefts of white wool around the legs, back, and head to smooth out the surface.

4 For the tail, make a small sausage (see page 9) measuring ¾ x ¼in (2 x 0.5cm) from white merino. Needle this onto the rear end (see page 11) as a base for the longer fluffy tail, which you will add later.

5 Cover the body with white alpaca. Wrap a wisp of fawn alpaca around the muzzle, fading it out up the head (see page 18). Needle a few patches of fawn alpaca onto the dog's back. Using light brown merino, make two flat triangles for the ears (see page 10) measuring 2in (5cm) long and ¾in (2cm) wide. Attach the tops of the floppy ears to the sides of the head (see page 21).

6 Add folded wisps of fawn alpaca and white merino to each ear, so that the insides and bottom of the outsides remain brown. Shade in the eye patches with chestnut-brown and a few strands of burnt orange. Needle in the eye sockets in the patches and create white almond-shaped eyes. Add chestnut-brown irises and white wool highlights (see page 20). Add an upside-down triangle of chestnut-brown for the nose and a thin strip for the mouth; start by needling on the middle of the strand under the nose and then guide the ends into place with the needle. Add a few folded wisps of blond silk fibers to the ears and the crown of the head (see page 20).

7 Needle together folded wisps of white alpaca and merino to make the tail shape (see page 9). Needle this onto the tail base, then hold the tail with one hand and needle all down the middle from base to tip, curling it a little with your fingers (see page 13). Add chestnut-brown lines to each paw to define the toes (see page 18).

TIP

Look at some photos of a Shetland pony if you want yours to have a different pose.

Perfect Pony

Shetland ponies are tiny, reaching up to 40 inches (1 meter) tall, and make great pets when learning to ride. There are many traditional markings and colorings that you can copy in felt, using natural, fluffy wool for their thick coats and silk fibers for their unruly manes and tails!

You will need

Carded sheep fleece in white 0.35oz (10g)

Merino wool in
white 0.70oz (20g)
peach 0.01oz (0.5g)
black 0.10oz (3g)

Alpaca wool in
chestnut-brown 0.35oz (10g)
white 0.18oz (5g)

Carded wool in mottled gray 0.01oz (0.5g)

Silk fibers in blond 0.18oz (5g)

Felting needle with handle

Foam block

Sharp embroidery scissors

Techniques Checklist

Basic Body 1 page 14
Padding Shapes page 13
Shaping Pieces page 13
Extending Shapes page 13
Applying Color page 18
Making Basic Shapes: Ears, Tails, and Wings page 10
Adding Ears page 21
Making an Eye page 20
Adding Fluffy Texture page 20

1 Make a Basic Body 1 (see page 14) from white carded fleece, making an egg-shaped body measuring 4in (10cm) long by 2⅝in (6.5cm) wide at the fattest point. Using the same wool, make the neck 2¾in (7cm) long and 1½in (4cm) wide at the base, and the head 2⅝ x 1¾in (6.5 x 4.5cm), making it a rounded tube shape as shown. Make the legs from white merino wool, making them 3in (8cm) long and ⅝in (1.5cm) thick. Attach them so that 2⅞in (7.5cm) hangs below the body, making sure that they are level so your pony won't topple.

2 Build up the thighs and haunches on the rear legs with a few curled wisps of white merino (see page 13). Bend the legs as shown and squeeze and needle the bends to hold them in place (see page 13). Pinch and shape the head with your needle to create the muzzle shape, then make it longer by wrapping a few wefts of white merino around the muzzle and needling into shape (see page 13).

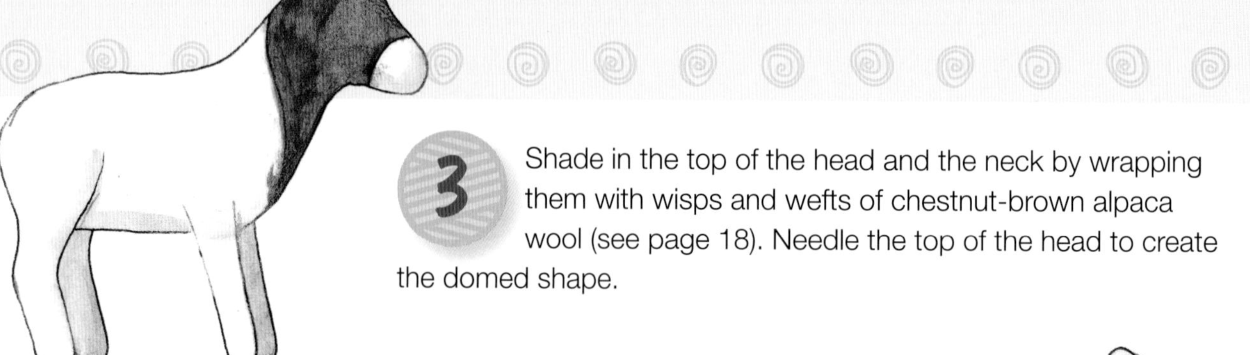

3 Shade in the top of the head and the neck by wrapping them with wisps and wefts of chestnut-brown alpaca wool (see page 18). Needle the top of the head to create the domed shape.

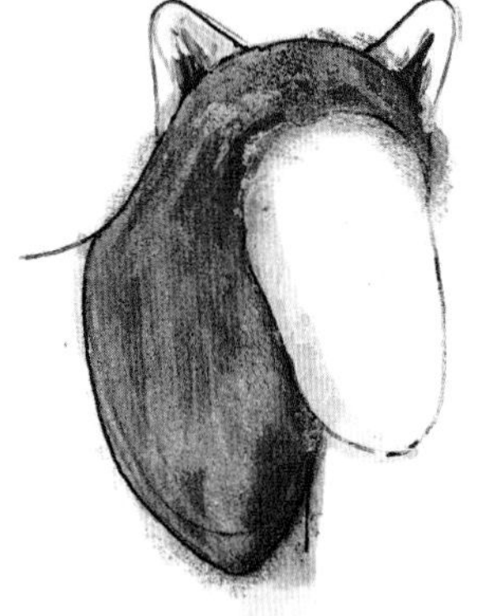

4 For the ears, use white merino wool to make two flat almond shapes on the foam block (see page 10), each measuring 1¼ x ¾in (3 x 2cm). Shade one side with chestnut-brown alpaca. Attach the ears in position, with the chestnut color on the back. Needle all around the base of each ear, then add a bit of chestnut alpaca to smooth the join on the back (see page 21). Add a triangle of peach and a little chestnut to the inside of each ear (see page 18).

5 Pad out the pony's rear end and tummy with wefts of the carded fleece (see page 13). Then cover the body with white merino to cover up the fleece and smooth the surface. Shade the rear of the pony with chestnut alpaca, leaving the front legs and a band across the shoulders white.

6 Squeeze in the sides of the body in between the legs and under the belly and needle them. Squeeze down the dip in the back and hold it in place with one hand, then needle the dip to keep the shape.

7 Wrap a wisp of black merino around the tip of each leg. Needle in the ankle to shape it, then flatten the bottom of the hoof by pressing it with your fingers and needling it. Work the needle into the back of the hoof to flatten it, leaving the front rounded. Check that the pony stands level on all four legs without wobbling.

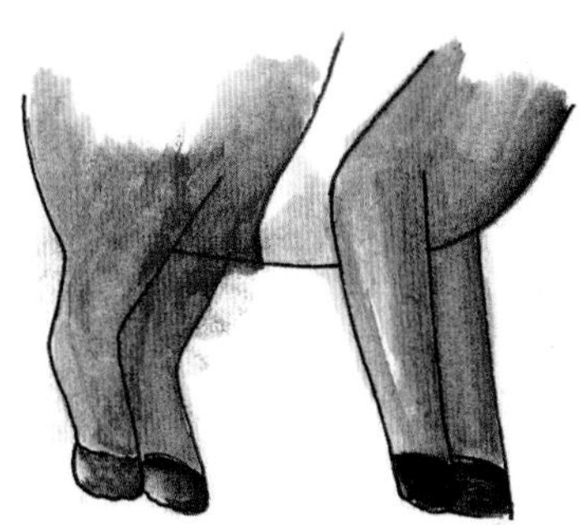

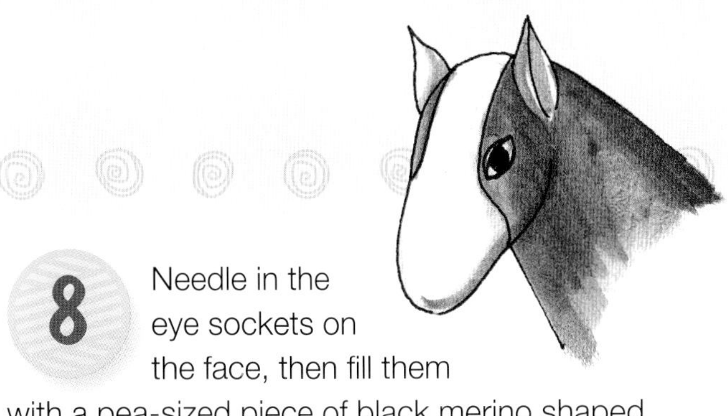

8 Needle in the eye sockets on the face, then fill them with a pea-sized piece of black merino shaped into an almond. Outline the eye with a thin strand of white merino and add a white highlight (see page 20). Add a wisp of white merino running from the white muzzle up to the top of the head (see page 18). Then add a wisp of gray carded wool running from between the eyes down to the mouth.

9 Add small almonds of black merino for the nostrils, then outline them with a sliver of white merino. Needle on a sliver of black merino for the mouth and a sliver of white merino directly above it for the top lip.

10 For the swishy mane, add a few folded wisps of white alpaca between the ears with the wispy ends making the forelock (see page 20); very lightly needle this to one side, so that you can see the pony's eyes. Add more folded wisps down the neck, with the folds in a line along the back of the neck and the ends hanging down on one side. Use the needle to guide any messy fibers into the mane.

SAFETY NOTE

As the mane and tail are quite loose, this felted animal should not be given as a toy to a child aged under three years old.

11 Add a few wefts of white alpaca to the pony's rear end, needling on one end of each weft and leaving the other end loose. Build up the tail so that it has lovely volume. Then add a few wisps of the blond silk fibers to the forelock, mane, and tail. Finish off by styling and trimming the hair with the scissors.

Dinky Dachshund

Dachshunds are small dogs with big characters! This little mutt has a fetching bandana, but you could make a collar from a strip of wool or attach a piece of ribbon instead. This project uses wet felting to smooth out the wool to give a perfect flat coat.

You will need

Merino wool in
chestnut-brown 0.70oz (20g)
charcoal-gray 0.18oz (5g)
gray 0.07oz (2g)
pink 0.01oz (0.5g)
black 0.01oz (0.5g)
peach 0.07oz (2g)
white 0.07oz (2g)
red 0.10oz (3g)

Felting needle with handle

Foam block

Sharp embroidery scissors

Liquid soap or dishwashing detergent (washing-up liquid)

Techniques Checklist

Basic Body 1 page 14
Padding Shapes page 13
Extending Shapes page 13
Shaping Pieces page 13
Applying Color page 18
Making Basic Shapes: Legs and Tails page 9
Joining Basic Shapes page 11
Making Basic Shapes: Ears, Tails, and Wings page 10
Making an Eye page 20

1 Make Basic Body 1 (see page 14), using chestnut-brown wool to make a long, very slim egg shape measuring 4½in (11cm) long by 1⅜in (3.5cm) wide at the fattest point for the body; the narrow end will be the base of the neck. Build the neck up until it measures 1⅜in (3.5cm) high. Make a small egg measuring 1¾ x 1in (4.5 x 2.5cm) for the head and join it to the top of the neck.

2 Build up the head, neck, and chest with wisps of brown wool (see page 13). Wrap a wisp around the neck and needle it on. Add a folded wisp across the back of the head to make it 1¼in (3cm) high, then wrap a wisp over the muzzle to enlarge it to ¾in (2cm) long (see page 13).

3 Make four legs, making each one 2¾in (7cm) long. Attach the front legs ⅜in (1cm) back from the chest with 2in (5cm) hanging below the body, and the back legs ¾in (2cm) in from the rear end with 1½in (6cm) hanging below—this gives your Dachshund a slightly raised rear end. Check that the feet are level.

Go FETCH!

4 Wrap a few wisps of brown wool around each leg join and around the lower parts of the legs and needle them to sculpt them into the posture shown in the photograph—this is known as a play bow. Bend over ¾in (2cm) of the tips of the legs and pinch and needle them to shape the paws (see page 13). Add charcoal-gray wool to the paws and ankles and a few strands of gray wool to each paw to define the toes (see page 18).

5 Fold a 3in (8cm) wisp of brown wool in half and felt it into a long, thin sausage shape (see page 9). Attach this tail to the dog's rear (see page 11) so that it curls up as shown, then use embroidery scissors to trim the tip into a point.

6 With the brown wool, create two flat, teardrop shapes measuring 1½ x ¾in (4 x 2cm) for the ears (see page 10). Add a few strands of pink and black around the bottom edges (see page 18). Attach the ears toward the back of the head (see page 21), blending them in with wisps of brown wool. Needle the top of the head to flatten it a little (see page 13).

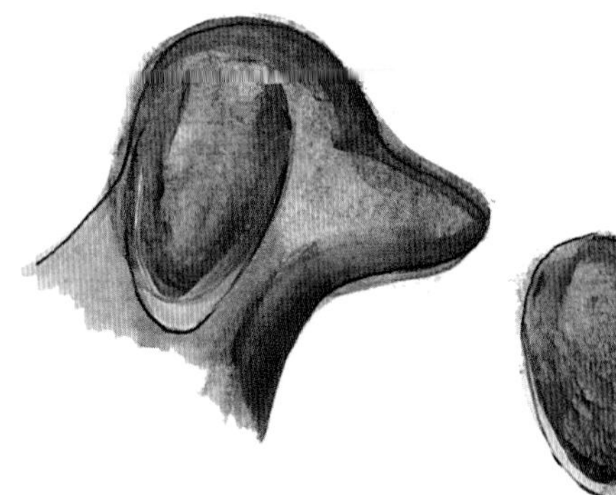

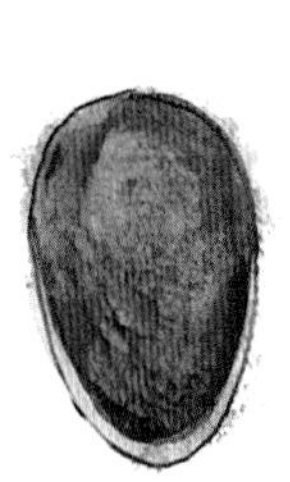

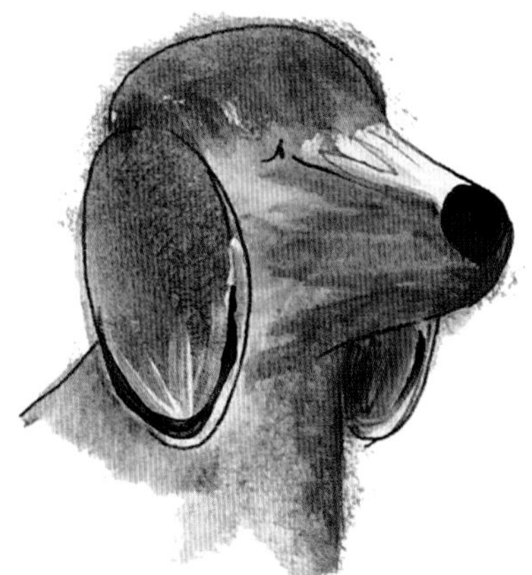

7 Add a little peach wool to the muzzle and needle black wool onto the tip to make the nose (see page 18). Needle in small dips for the eye sockets, shaping the ridge above the eyes at the same time (see page 13).

8 Add a pea-sized ball of black wool in each socket for the eyes. Add a small dot of white wool for the highlight in each eye, and peach wool eyelids (see page 20). Check that the eyes are level when seen from the front.

9 On the foam block make the red bandana: this is a flat triangle (see page 10) with longer sides to wrap around the neck, with a bit of white wool to make the heart shape in the center, as shown (see page 18).

10 Wet felt the bandana and the dog by wetting the pieces with a little warm water and then rubbing on a bit of liquid soap or dishwashing detergent. Rub the bandana with your fingers until it feels completely felted and smooth. Then rub your fingers all over the curves of the dog, but do not overwork the piece as it might shrink too much: you just want to give the dog a smooth finish. Rinse the soap off both pieces and dry them in warm place like an airing cupboard or near a radiator.

11 Wrap the bandana around the dog's neck and felt the ends together with the felting needle to hold it in place.

Beautiful Bunny

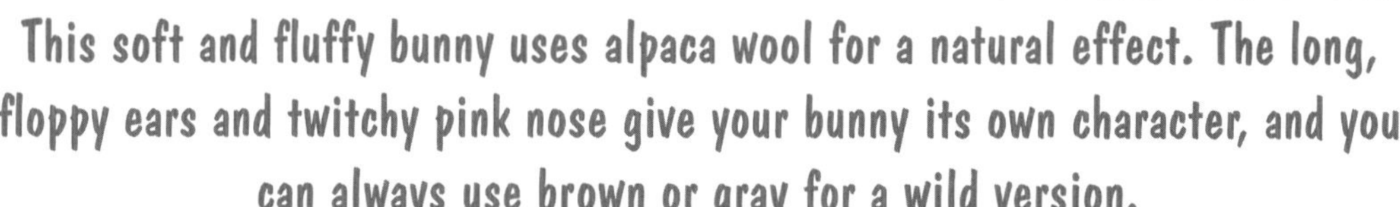

This soft and fluffy bunny uses alpaca wool for a natural effect. The long, floppy ears and twitchy pink nose give your bunny its own character, and you can always use brown or gray for a wild version.

You will need

Merino wool in
white 0.70oz (20g)
light brown 0.10oz (3g)
dark pink 0.18oz (5g)
black 0.07oz (2g)
yellow 0.01oz (0.5g)
gray 0.01oz (0.5g)

Carded wool in
dark brown 0.35oz (10g)
mottled gray 0.35oz (10g)

Alpaca wool in white 0.35oz (10g)

Felting needle with handle

Foam block

Sharp embroidery scissors

Techniques Checklist

Making Basic Shapes: Bodies and Heads page 8
Joining Basic Shapes page 11
Blending Joined Shapes page 12
Basic Body 2 page 15
Shaping Pieces page 13
Applying Color page 18
Padding Shapes page 13
Adding Fluffy Texture page 20
Making Basic Shapes: Ears, Tails, and Wings page 10
Adding Ears page 21
Making an Eye page 20

1 Using white merino wool, make a Basic Body 2 (see page 15), making an egg-shaped body measuring 3¼in (8.5cm) long by 2in (5cm) wide at the fattest point. Make a head measuring 2½ x 1⅜in (6 x 3.5cm) from the same wool and a ball ⅝in (1.5cm) in diameter (see page 8). Join the ball to one end of the head (see page 11). Wrap the join with a weft of white to blend the pieces into the shape shown (see page 12).

2 Follow Basic Body 2 to attach the head to the body and to make and attach the legs. Make four legs measuring 2¾ x ⅜in (7 x 1cm) from white wool. Attach the front legs at an angle ⅜in (1cm) down from the jaw, as shown. Bend over the tips of the legs by ⅜in (1cm) and pinch and needle into position for the paws (see page 13).

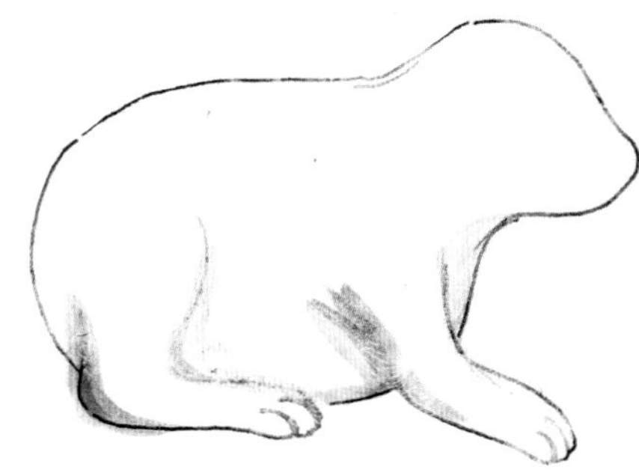

3 Attach the back legs at the tops, then bend them into shape with a right angle at the join, and needle in around the bend until it is firmly held in place. Add a few strands of gray to each paw to define the toes (see page 18).

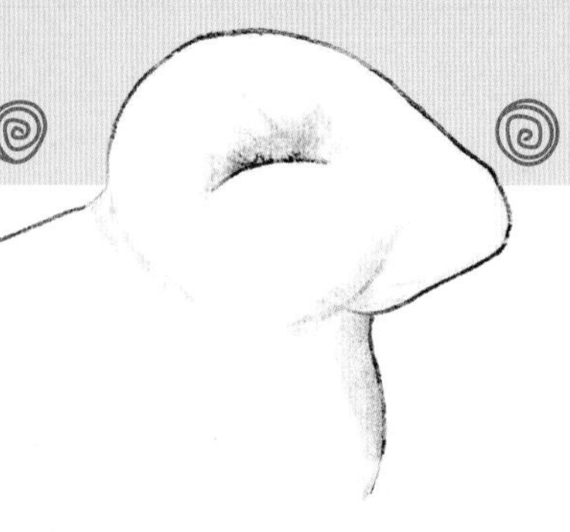

4 Add 1¼-in (3-cm) ovals of white wool to the cheeks, needling them in around the edges (see page 13). Needle in above the cheek to create a dip for the eye sockets on both sides, then pinch and needle in the shape of the nose (see page 13).

5 Add a weft of white wool over the back to blend in the back leg joins and build up the roundedness of the body, then add a wisp of white wool to build up the haunches and shoulders of the back and front legs. Add a weft of white wool to the chest to build up the shape.

6 Curl a wisp of white wool into a pillow shape and attach it to the rear end for the tail. Needle it on, then add a few wisps of white alpaca wool to give it a soft and fluffy texture (see page 20).

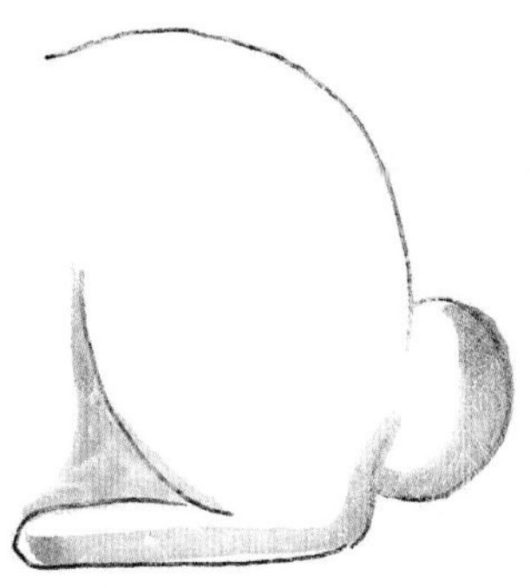

7 From mottled gray wool, make two flat ovals for the ears (see page 10), measuring 2½ x 1in (6 x 2.5cm). Using the embroidery scissors, trim them into the shape shown in the photograph. Add a few strands of light brown merino to the outer side of each ear and small, short wisps of dark pink to the inners.

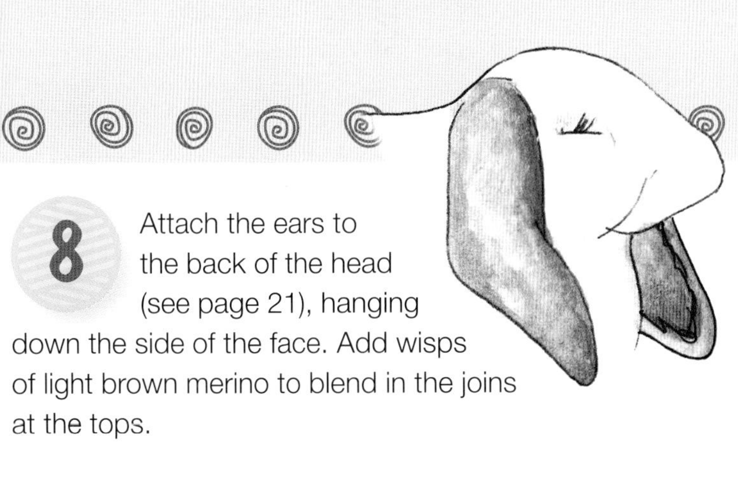

8 Attach the ears to the back of the head (see page 21), hanging down the side of the face. Add wisps of light brown merino to blend in the joins at the tops.

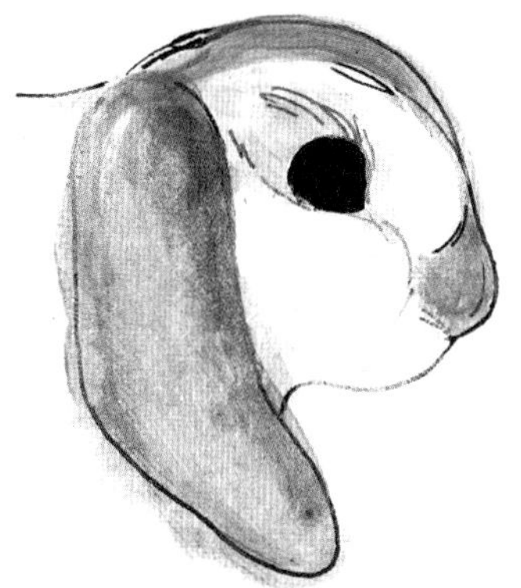

9 Add a pea-sized piece of black merino for the eye in the sockets. Add a few strands of light brown, yellow, and gray merino to the rabbit's muzzle, extending them up to the crown. Shape the head further by needling in the indent of the mouth. Add short wisps of white alpaca to the head and body to give your rabbit a soft, cuddly finish.

10 Using black merino, extend the eye into an almond shape, then add a few strands of white merino for the highlight (see page 20). Add a strand of light brown merino above the eye to create the eyelid, then outline the top edge of the eye with white merino.

11 For the nose, add a few strands of black to the end of the muzzle, then add a line of dark pink above the black (see page 18). Use a sliver of dark pink for the mouth; start by needling on the middle of the strand just under the nose and then guide the ends into place with the needle.

With a HOP, a SKIP, and a JUMP!

Super-Cute Yorkie

This little terrier is fresh from the grooming parlor, with a pretty ribbon topknot and beautifully styled fur. Because the wool fibers are kept fluffy, the body shape is hidden, so you don't need to worry too much if the shape isn't perfect!

You will need

Carded top wool in mottled gray 0.18oz (5g)

Alpaca wool in
beige 0.07oz (2g)
white 0.07oz (2g)

Merino wool in
brown 0.07oz (2g)
black 0.03oz (1g)
golden yellow 0.07oz (2g)
light yellow 0.07oz (2g)
peach 0.10oz (3g)

Silk fibers in
gray and black mix 0.18oz (5g)
light blond 0.10oz (3g)

Felting needle with handle

Foam block

Sharp embroidery scissors

Two shiny ⅛in (3mm) black beads

Fabric glue

Beading needle and black thread (optional)

Thin red ribbon or fabric strip 4in (10cm) long

Techniques Checklist

Basic Body 2 page 15
Shaping Pieces page 13
Blending Joined Shapes page 12
Extending Shapes page 13
Applying Color page 18
Adding Fluffy Texture page 20
Making Basic Shapes: Ears, Tails, and Wings page 10
Adding Ears page 21

1 From gray carded wool make a Basic Body 2 (see page 15), making an egg-shaped body measuring 2⅝in (6.5cm) long by 1⅜in (3.5cm) wide at the fattest point. Make a head measuring 1½ x 1¼in (4 x 3cm) from the same wool, making it the pointed shape shown.

2 Make four legs, each from a weft of beige alpaca mixed with a wisp of gray carded wool. Make the legs 2¾in (7cm) long and ⅜in (1cm) thick. Bend over ⅜in (1cm) on the front legs and ⅝in (1.5cm) on the back legs to make paws, and needle them into position (see page 13). Attach the legs to the body as shown, so that the tummy is about ⅝in (1.5cm) off the ground and the dog stands level without toppling.

3 Add wisps of gray wool to cover the top of each leg and to blend in the joins (see page 12). Shape the muzzle by pinching it into a point and needling it (see page 13). Add some brown wool to the muzzle to enlarge it to the shape shown (see page 13). Keep needling the chest area and under the chin until they are firm.

4 For the fur, add a thin layer of black wool over the dog's back for a base color and a folded weft of white alpaca on the chest, running down to the tummy (see page 18). To give height and base color to the head, add folded wisps of golden yellow and light yellow merino to the top of the head, with the folded ends either side of a middle parting and the wispy ends hanging down the sides of the head.

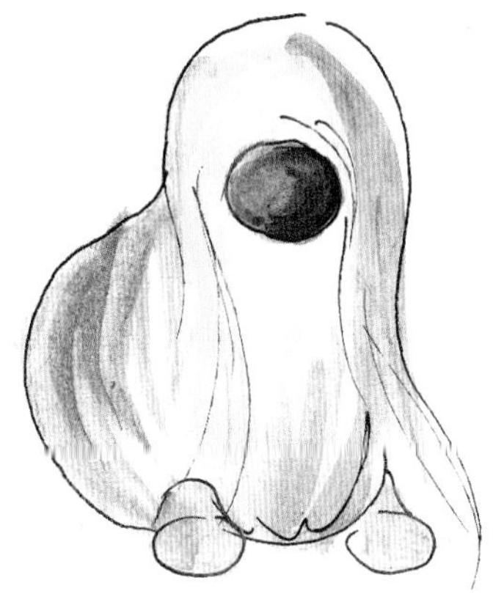

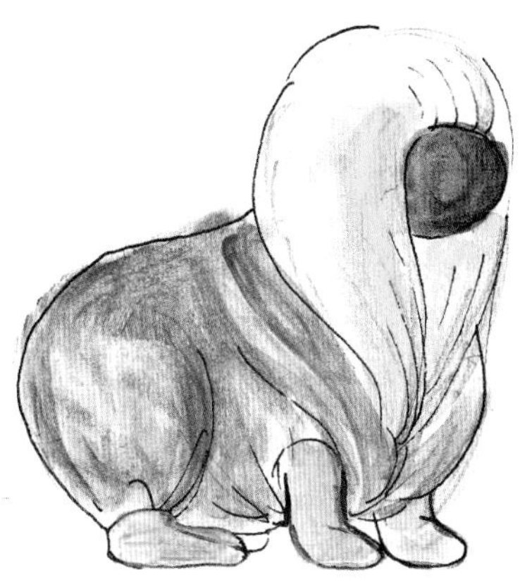

5 Lay gray and black mix silk fibers over the dog's back. Needle all these fibers on lightly to keep the hair soft and wispy (see page 20) and wrap them around the body as shown. Then add wisps of light blond silk fibers, keeping the fibers long and sweeping them back from the top of the muzzle over the head.

6 From peach wool make two teardrops for the ears (see page 10), measuring ¾ x ⅜in (2 x 1cm). Add wisps of brown wool to give a mottled finish with the peach showing through (see page 18).

BEST in show!

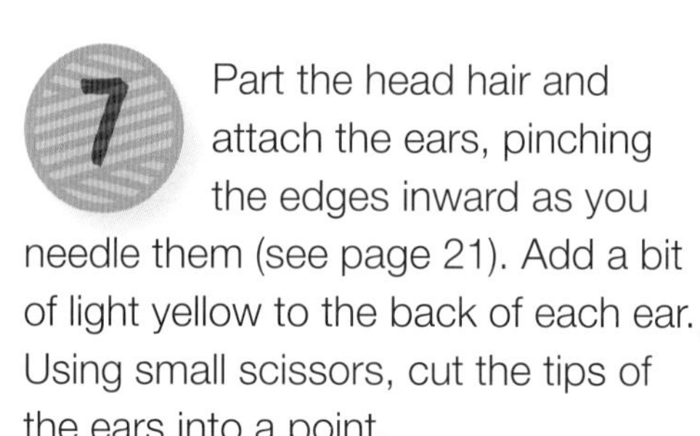

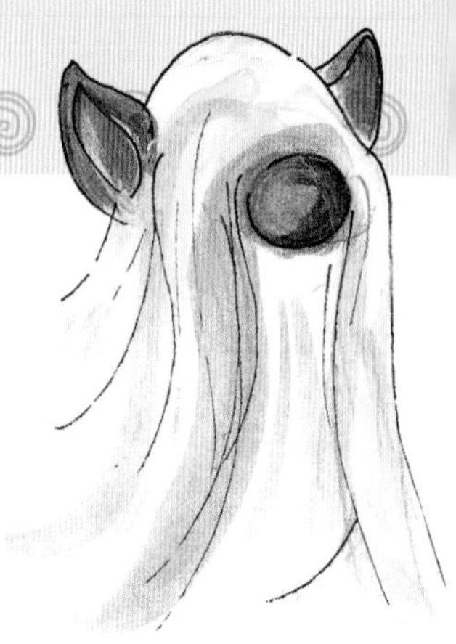

7 Part the head hair and attach the ears, pinching the edges inward as you needle them (see page 21). Add a bit of light yellow to the back of each ear. Using small scissors, cut the tips of the ears into a point.

8 For the eyes, you can either glue the beads into place with fabric glue, or sew them on. If sewing, use a beading needle and insert it underneath the chin so that the knot can be hidden. Carefully push the needle through the head to where you would like the eye to go, thread on a black bead, and insert the needle back down through the head to the starting point. Repeat for the other eye. Finish by making a knot under the chin. Cover up the knot with a bit of brown wool and white alpaca.

9 Needle on an upside-down triangle of black wool for the nose (see page 18). Add a bit of golden yellow wool to the muzzle, just under the eyes, needling the wisps on down the center of the muzzle, then add a few wisps of brown and yellow. Build up the hair above the eyes to give the dog a cute expression.

10 For the topknot, take a long, folded wisp of blond silk fibers and attach just the fold to the top of the muzzle. Wrap the loose ends of the fibers over the top of the head. Then use the thin red ribbon or fabric strip to tie a bow around it at the top of the head. Lightly needle the loose silk fibers down the back of the head and around the shoulders to the front, so that they do not spread onto the gray back. Trim all the hair, using the photographs as a guide.

Pug Puppy

With their wrinkled faces and big round eyes, pug puppies are utterly adorable. There's lots of needling in this project to get that particular pug expression but it's worth it!

You will need

Carded wool in
white/cream 0.90oz (25g)
dark brown 0.18oz (5g)
oatmeal 0.18oz (5g)
gray 0.07oz (2g)
black 0.18oz (5g)
reddish-brown 0.03oz (1g)

Alpaca wool in fawn 0.70oz (20g)

Felting needle with handle

Foam block

Sharp embroidery scissors

Thin strip of red leather, ribbon, or ready-made felt for collar

Gold-colored bead big enough to thread onto collar

Fabric glue

Techniques Checklist

Basic Body 2 page 15
Shaping Pieces page 13
Padding Shapes page 13
Joining Basic Shapes page 11
Blending Joined Shapes page 12
Applying Color page 18
Making Basic Shapes: Legs and Tails page 9
Making Basic Shapes: Ears, Tails, and Wings page 10
Adding Ears page 21
Padding Shapes page 13
Making an Eye page 20

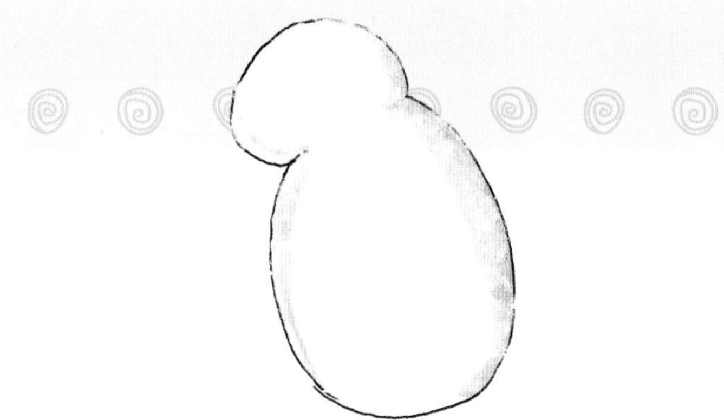

1 Follow the first stages of Basic Body 2 (see page 15), using white wool to make an egg-shaped body measuring 2½in (6cm) long by 1¾in (4.5cm) wide at the fattest point. Make a head measuring 2 x 1¾in (5 x 4.5cm) from the same wool, attaching it to the top of the narrow end of the body, as shown.

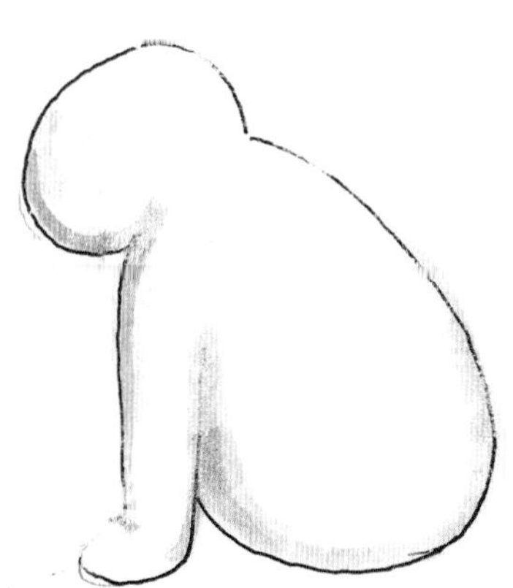

2 Make two legs measuring 2½in (6cm) long by ⅝in (1.5cm) thick from white wool. Bend over ⅜in (1cm) at one end for the paws and pinch the heels while you needle them to hold them in that position (see page 13). Add a little more wool to the paws (see page 13) to make them rounder. Hold the body upright and attach the legs to the shoulders, as shown (see page 11), so that your pug is sitting.

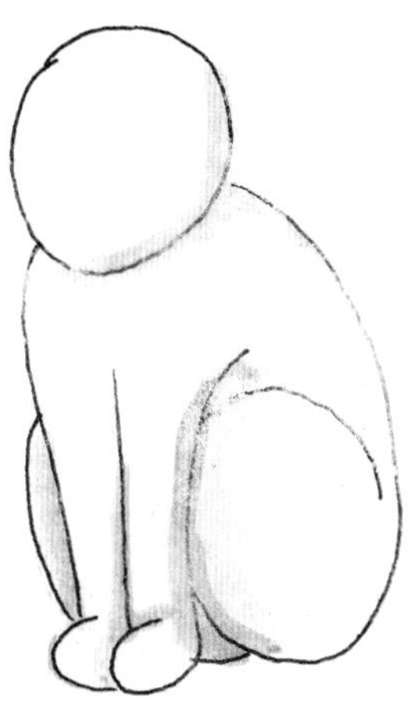

3 For the back legs, add a soft ball of white wool measuring 1⅜ x 1½in (3.5 x 4cm) (see page 13) to each side of the lower body for the haunches. Needle the balls on around the edges, being careful not to flatten them. Needle in deeply around the top and front of the balls where they join the body so that the haunch crease is defined.

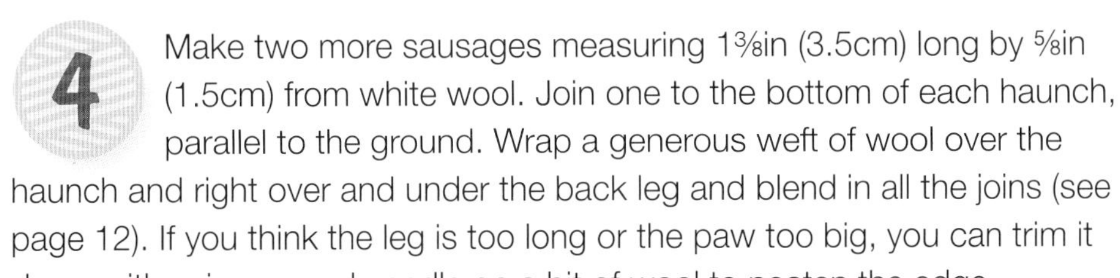

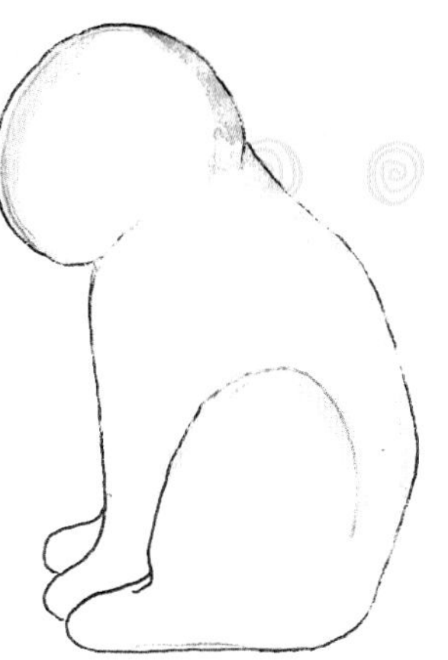

4 Make two more sausages measuring 1⅜in (3.5cm) long by ⅝in (1.5cm) from white wool. Join one to the bottom of each haunch, parallel to the ground. Wrap a generous weft of wool over the haunch and right over and under the back leg and blend in all the joins (see page 12). If you think the leg is too long or the paw too big, you can trim it down with scissors and needle on a bit of wool to neaten the edge.

5 Make a soft ball measuring ¾ x 1⅜in (2 x 3.5cm) from dark brown wool for the muzzle. Attach it to the front of the head in the same way as for the haunch, needling around the edges and keeping the shape very rounded, as shown.

6 Cover the whole dog with fawn alpaca wool (see page 18), except the tips of the paws and the muzzle. Use the fawn wool to blend in the join between the front legs and the body (see page 12) and to fill out the puppy's rear end a little.

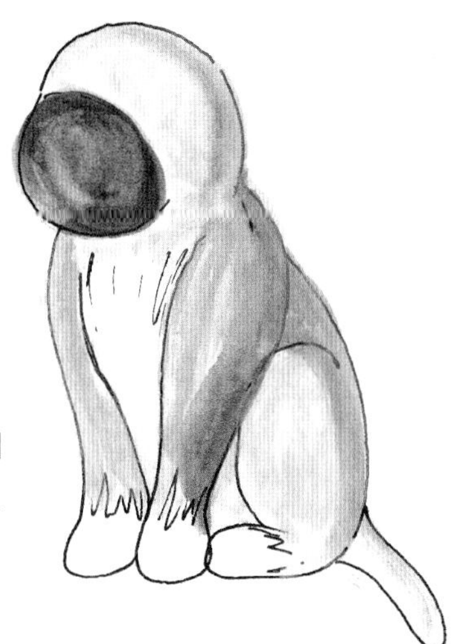

7 For the tail, make a sausage (see page 9) measuring 2¾ x ⅜in (7 x 1cm) from white wool and cover it with fawn alpaca. Attach it to the pug's rear end using a weft of fawn wool (see page 11), but do not curl it up yet.

8 From dark brown wool, make two flat triangles (see page 10) measuring 1 x 1⅜in (2.5 x 3.5cm). Position one edge of each triangle on each side of the head, with the tip of the ear pointing toward the nose, and attach it just along the top edge. Lift the ear a little, so that you can see the underside when looking at the pug's face, and needle around the back of the ear to hold it in this position (see page 21).

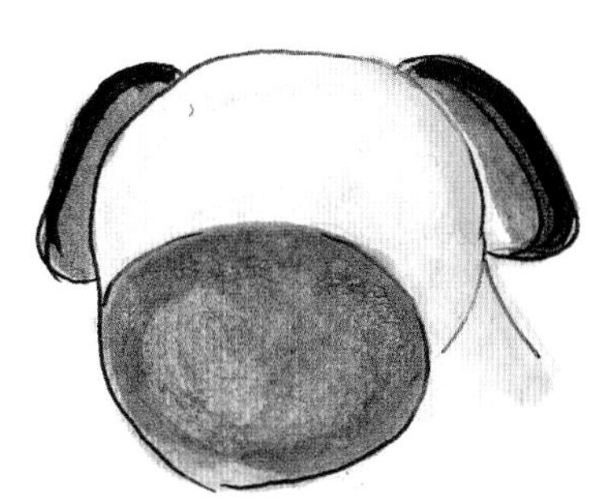

9 Shade the back of the ears with fawn alpaca, followed by oatmeal and gray wool toward the tip. Then add a weft of the fawn alpaca to the back of the head over the base of the ears to build up the shape of the head and to give it a smoother finish.

10 Build up the cheeks a little with dark brown wool (see page 13). Make a thin sausage of mixed oatmeal and gray wool and lay it along the join between the muzzle and the head. Needle it on, keeping it slightly rounded to make the wrinkles above the pug's nose (see page 18). Outline the nose and mouth with black wool and needle over the lines until they are indented and the nose protrudes.

11 Shade in the areas where the eyes will be with a little gray wool, then add large almonds of white wool for the eyes (see page 20). Use the reddish-brown wool to make the irises, making them large so that just the white in the corners shows. Add black pupils and white highlights. Outline the eyes in black, making the top line thicker than the bottom one, then add a wisp of white for the eyelids and one of gray for the eyebrows.

12 Add some thin strips of oatmeal and gray to the forehead and crown area for the wrinkles above the eyes. Keep needling deeply over the lines while pinching with your fingers to make creases (see page 13). Pull apart the fibers of a few wisps of gray wool and lightly needle them over the muzzle, then add a bit of white to the chin and the wrinkle above of the nose. For the whisker dots, add some small, thin strips of black wool, and finally add two small black dots for nostrils (see page 19).

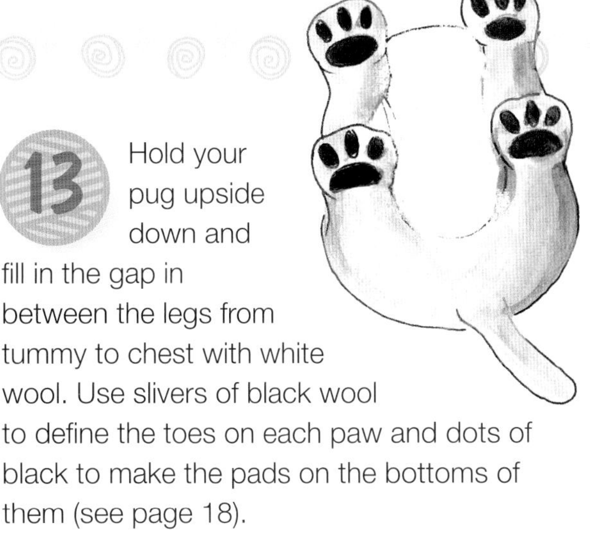

13 Hold your pug upside down and fill in the gap in between the legs from tummy to chest with white wool. Use slivers of black wool to define the toes on each paw and dots of black to make the pads on the bottoms of them (see page 18).

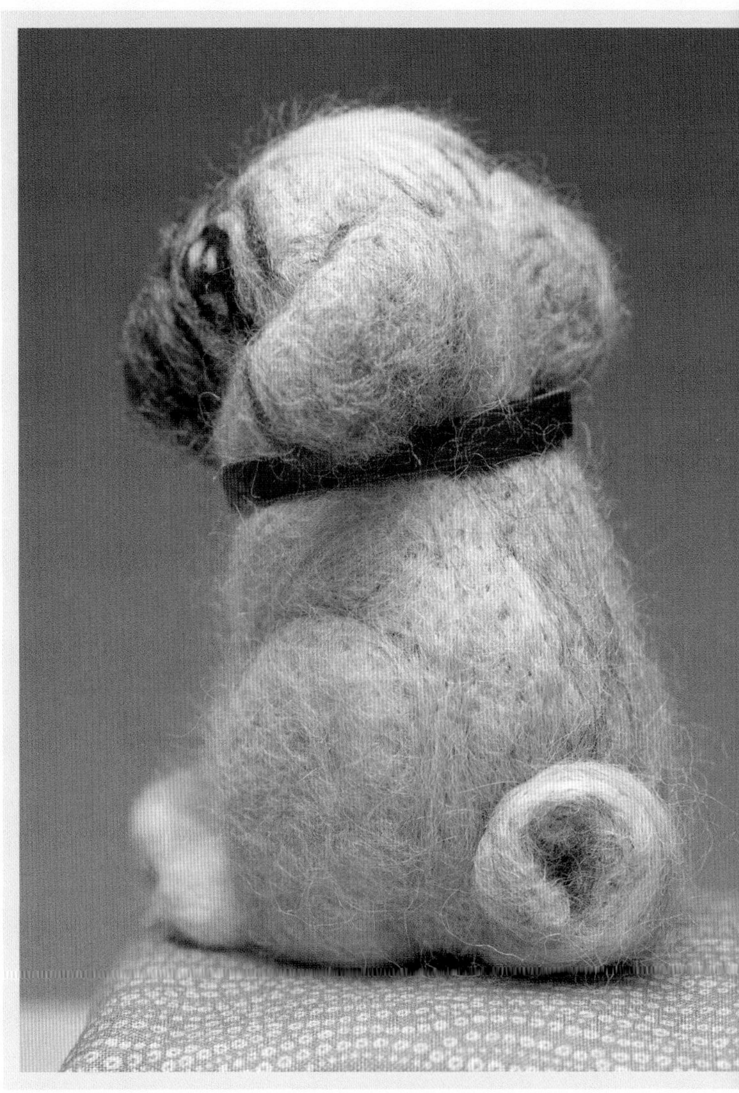

14 Curl up the tail, hold it in place with one hand, and needle it onto the back of the pug. Make sure the shape stays defined and doesn't blend into the body; you only need to needle it enough to hold it in position.

15 For the collar, thread the bead onto the strip of leather or felt, then glue the ends together around the pug's neck. He's ready for his first walk!

TIP

Try to give your pug's tail two curls, just like the real thing.

WALKIES!

TIP

Change the colors to oranges and yellows to make a marmalade kitten!

Playful Kitten

There's lots of color blending and mixing in this project to build up the kitten's fluffy fur and add her tabby markings. We've given her a sparkly collar made from beads, but you could use a piece of velvet ribbon instead, if you prefer.

You will need

Merino wool in
white 0.70oz (20g)
light brown 0.18oz (5g)
peach 0.07oz (2g)
bright blue 0.07oz (2g)
charcoal-black 0.35oz (10g)
dark brown 0.18oz (5g)

Alpaca fleece in
mottled light beige 0.35oz (10g)
white 0.18oz (5g)

Felting needle with handle

Foam block

Sharp embroidery scissors

Black cotton thread and beading needle (optional)

Silver-lined clear glass seed beads (optional)

Techniques Checklist

Basic Body 2 page 15
Shaping Pieces page 13
Padding Shapes page 13
Making Basic Shapes: Ears, Tails, and Wings page 10
Adding Ears page 21
Making an Eye page 20
Applying Color page 18
Joining Basic Shapes page 11
Blending Joined Shapes page 12
Adding Fluffy Texture page 20

1 From white merino wool make a Basic Body 2 (see page 15), making an egg-shaped body measuring 2¾in (7cm) long by 1½in (4cm) wide at the fattest point. Make an oval head measuring 1 x 1¼in (2.5 x 3cm) from the same wool.

2 Make the legs 2¾in (7cm) long and ⅜in (1cm) thick. Bend over ⅝in (1.5cm) of each leg and needle it into position to make the paw. Holding the body upright, attach the front legs as shown, just behind the neck and angled forward and inward, so that the paws touch.

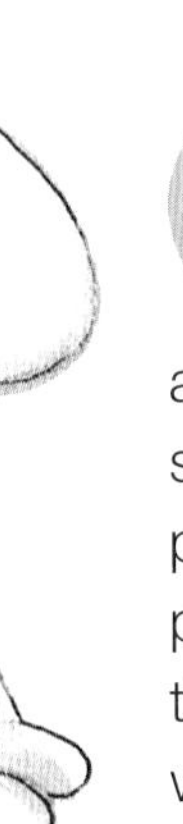

3 Attach the back legs to the sides of the body, as shown. Make the bend for the knee after you have needled the leg on, then squeeze and needle the bend to hold the position (see page 13). Angle the paws to point outward at 45 degrees and needle those in place. The kitten should sit up with all four paws on the ground.

Here kitty, kitty, KITTY!

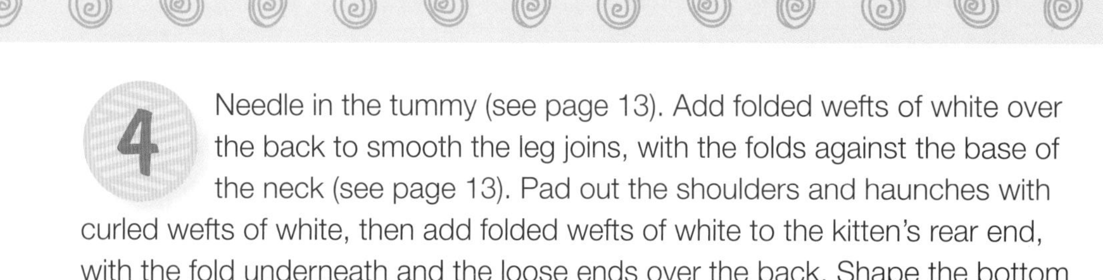
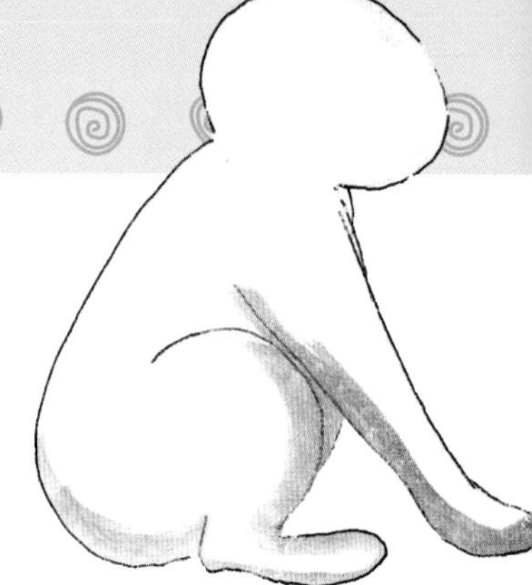

4 Needle in the tummy (see page 13). Add folded wefts of white over the back to smooth the leg joins, with the folds against the base of the neck (see page 13). Pad out the shoulders and haunches with curled wefts of white, then add folded wefts of white to the kitten's rear end, with the fold underneath and the loose ends over the back. Shape the bottom so that the kitten sits upright, and reposition the paws if you need to.

5 Pad out the head with folded wefts of white wool: a kitten's head is bigger in proportion to the body than an older cat's. Add a bit of white wool to pad out the mouth area.

6 Needle in the eye sockets, then pinch and needle the nose (see page 13). For the ears, use white merino to make two triangles measuring 1in (2.5cm) wide and 1⅜in (3.5cm) high (see page 10). Shade the ears with light brown on one side and peach on the other. Attach them tilting out at 45 degrees (see page 21), making sure they are level. Add light brown to blend the joins.

7 Needle a pea-sized piece of blue wool into an almond in each eye socket and outline it with charcoal. At the inner corner, extend the line toward the nose (see page 20). Add dark brown stripes over the head and peach yarn to the nose, between the eyes (see page 18).

8 Make sure the paws are touching; squeeze and needle the front legs in again if they have separated. Cover the body with mottled beige alpaca wool, leaving just the paws and the muzzle area uncovered (see page 18). Keep the wool loose to soften the shape of the haunches and cover the tops of the front legs.

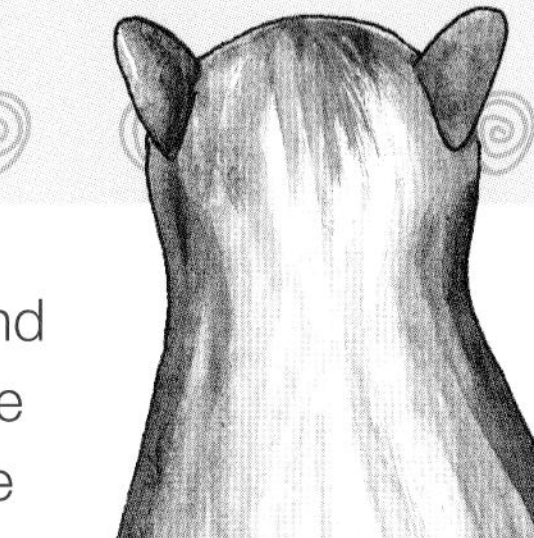

9 For the tail, make a stack with a weft each of beige alpaca, charcoal, dark brown, and a second weft of beige alpaca. Dampen your hands with warm water, then rub the stack between them to make a sausage. Needle short wisps of charcoal to one end, shaping the wisps to a soft point. With the scissors, cut off the other end to make the tail about 3½in (9cm) long.

10 Attach the cut end to the base of the kitten's back (see page 11), then bend it around to one side and needle it into position. Add beige alpaca to blend in the tail join (see page 12).

11 Shade in the chest with white merino and a bit of white alpaca, keeping it soft and fluffy (see page 20). Add short wisps of light brown, dark brown, and charcoal wool in soft stripes (see page 18) all over the body to make the tabby markings; use the photographs as a guide. Add a few short, thin strips of charcoal wool to each paw to define the toes.

12 Finish by adding fine detail to the face. Add a short strip of black to the top of each eye to strengthen the outline. Then add a white outline outside the black one. Add a black pupil at the top of the blue, so that it touches the eyelid, and a white highlight (see page 20). Needle on an upside-down triangle in brown for the nose. Use a sliver of brown for the mouth; start by needling on the middle of the strand under the nose, and then guide the ends into place.

13 If you'd like to make a glamorous collar, thread beads onto a length of black thread and tie it around the neck. Knot the ends firmly, then trim them.

Templates

All the templates used in the book are shown below at their actual size. Simply photocopy or scan the image at 100% onto a sheet of paper, and follow the instructions in the project.

Panda Patch
page 24 (100%)

Leopard Patch
page 26 (100%)

Cool Cat Brooch
page 92 (100%)

Dashing Dog Brooch
page 97 (100%)

Index

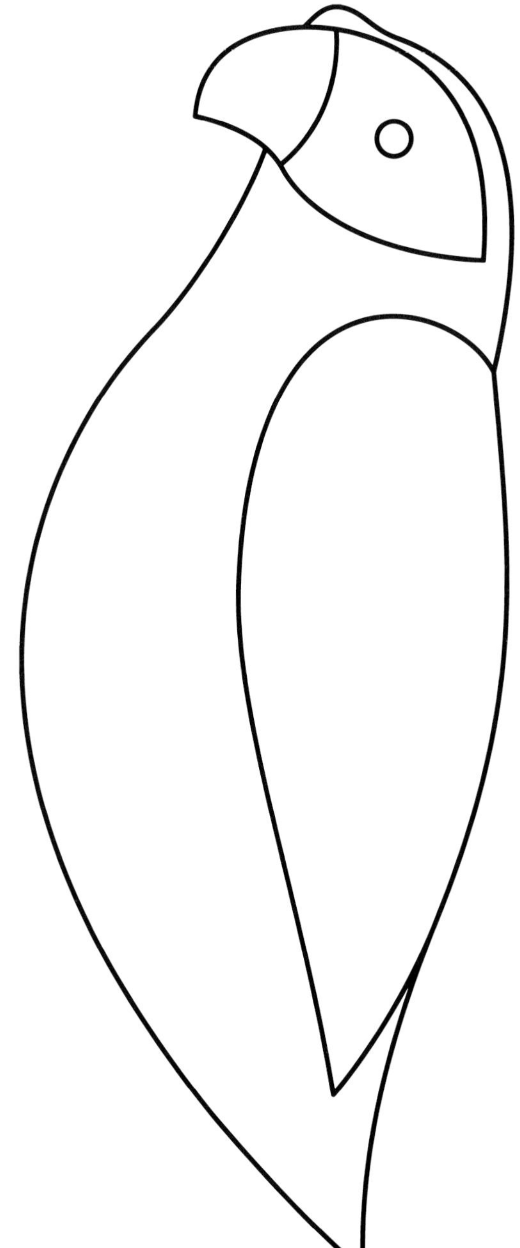

Colorful Parrot
page 64 (100%)

Suppliers

USA

A C Moore
www.acmoore.com

Darice
www.darice.com

Hobby Lobby
www.hobbylobby.com

Jo-ann Fabric & Crafts
www.joann.com

Michaels
www.michaels.com

Sarafina Fiber Art
www.sarafinafiberart.com

UK

Blooming Felt
www.bloomingfelt.co.uk

Homecrafts
www.homecrafts.co.uk

Hobbycraft
www.hobbycraft.co.uk

John Lewis
www.johnlewis.com